Come Follow Me
through the Old Testament

OTHER BOOKS BY SCOTT SORENSEN

Come Follow Me through the Book of Mormon

Come Follow Me through the Doctrine and Covenants

Come Follow Me through the Old Testament

Real Talk, Real Life Journal: Doctrine and Covenants

Real Talk, Real Life Journal: Old Testament

COME
FOLLOW
ME

through the
Old Testament

SCOTT SORENSEN

Covenant Communications, Inc.

To my parents, Tom and Sue Sorensen, for their love, support, and other-worldly belief in me.

INTRODUCTION

We are about to embark on a one-year journey through the Old Testament. Scary, right? This reminds me of a story from the Book of Mormon that would be better suited to the Old Testament. Soon after the events surrounding the Towel of Babel, a small group of people who valued their covenants and the words of prophets were led to safety. Their leader was a prophet referred to as "The brother of Jared . . . a man highly favored of the Lord."[1] A few years after their escape, the brother of Jared was commanded to build barges and cross a great sea with a "furious wind . . . mountain waves . . . great and terrible tempests," and even a "monsters of the sea."[2] With trust in the Lord as their steering mechanism, these twenty-two courageous souls, in eight barges, commended "themselves unto the Lord their God."[3]

This ancient story feels like a metaphor as I consider individuals' and families' courageous anticipation to "commend ourselves unto the Lord" in studying the Old Testament for an entire year. Studying this ancient book can feel like crossing a massive sea. As you anticipate this crossing, can you see mountain waves and furious winds? Can you already see the great and terrible tempest that will probably arise in your family? The more I look at the Jaredite experience, the more I can find similarities. In fact, it took them three hundred forty-four days—almost a year—to cross this sea![4]

My intention is to make this less of an introduction and more of a pep talk. Even though the Jaredites were letting God prevail, their lives did not get easier. "Many times [they were] buried in the depths of the sea."[5] What allowed them to continue and not give up? After particularly difficult days, weeks, even months experiencing deep water and winds that never ceased, what motivated them to keep going? Here are three simple principles we learn from the Jaredites:

First, *always find the light*. No matter how dark it was or how deep they were buried, they still had light in their vessels.[6] As you study this year, please take time to recognize the light in your life. Your purpose this year is not necessarily to read everything but to find ways to bring a little light into your life each day.

Second, *you can't control the waves, but you can control your praise*. Whether they were having a good day or a rough day, the Jaredites "did sing praises unto the Lord; the brother of Jared did sing praises unto the Lord, and he did thank and praise the Lord all the day long; and when the night came, they did not cease to praise the Lord."[7] You may not always be grateful for what 2022 has in store, but giving praise to God that He can get you where you need to go is crucial.

Third, *always look for the personality and character of Christ*. The barges in this story take on specific characteristics of Christ. They are "tight like unto a dish,"[8] wherefore, the Jaredites knew that when they were buried under mountain waves, "there was no water could hurt them, their vessels being tight like unto a

---

1 Ether 1:33–34.
2 Ether 6:5–10.
3 Ether 6:4.
4 Ether 6:11.
5 Ether 6:6.
6 See Ether 6:1; something similar happened to the Israelites in Egypt during three days of darkness (see Exodus 10:21–24).
7 Ether 6:9.
8 Ether 2:17; 6:7.

dish." Just as they knew they could trust in their vessels, a consistent study of the Old Testament will reveal Jesus to you in ways that will strengthen your desire to choose to trust in Him. Even though it will get rough at times, you can trust in His power to help you.

Finally, let me tell you about a time when I legitimately felt the Holy Ghost while watching college football fifteen years ago. Retired Notre Dame head football coach Lou Holtz was giving viewers a glimpse into some of the important pep talks he gave his team as they approached extremely difficult and pressure-packed games. Coach Holtz told them to focus only on one simple thing. "Do whatever it takes to W.I.N." Then he went on to explain that W.I.N. stands for "What's Important Now?" That's the pep talk I would give you as you study the Old Testament. Ask yourself, your study group, and your Heavenly Father, "What's important now in my *Come Follow Me* study?" If you've missed a few days, weeks, or months, simply start now.

My hope is that the word of the Lord will be "a lamp unto [our] feet, and a light unto [our] path"[9] as we study the Old Testament this year.

Let's go!

---

9 Psalms 119:105.

DECEMBER 27–JANUARY 2
"THIS IS MY WORK AND MY GLORY"
MOSES 1; ABRAHAM 3

God's Message to Me from This Section

"FULL OF EYES" (10 MINUTES)

How many eyes do you think each of the following creatures has?

A. Praying mantis _____

B. Jumping spider _____

C. Box jellyfish _____

D. Starfish _____

(Answers: A: 5 eyes; B: 8 eyes; C: 24 eyes; D: 5+ eyes [they usually have 1 eye for each arm])

Welcome to the Old Testament! You will quickly notice the writing style and tone of the Old Testament is far different from the Doctrine and Covenants. This makes sense because "the Lord God . . . speaketh unto men according to *their* language, unto *their* understanding."[10] In both the Old and New Testament, the writing is more poetic, symbolic, and multilayered. For example, both John the Beloved and Ezekiel had visions where they saw heavenly beings who they partly described as being "full of eyes."[11] The basic symbolism is to teach that these beings are full of light and knowledge. In other words, they are full of vision and light! Moses 1 and Abraham 3 are examples of how God works with His followers to fill them with eyes!

---

10 2 Nephi 31:3, *emphasis added.*

11 Ezekiel 1:18; 10:12; Revelations 4:6.

Who do you know who is "full of eyes," meaning they seem to have heavenly wisdom and understanding?

Moses saw "God face to face" (Moses 1:2); what can God see? Read Moses 1:3–6 and notice all that God can see. A significant attribute of God is that He is "full of eyes." God is also:

- "Almighty"

- "Endless"

- The Creator of "works . . . without end, and also . . . words, for they never cease"

- Omnipresent and omniscient ("All things are present with [Him], for [He knows] them all.")

But what else does God see? Read Moses 1:3-6 again.

- That Moses is *His son*, and God has a work for him!

Why do you think God wanted Moses to know that Moses worships a very *big* God?

What are some characteristics of God that are hard for you to understand sometimes?

WHY DID GOD CREATE ALL OF THIS? (20 MINUTES)

Remember the reason we have the book of Moses. As Joseph Smith was making inspired revisions to the Bible, he began with Genesis in the Old Testament.

Joseph quickly learned there was so much of Moses's writings missing that he had to restore full chapters. The result is the book of Moses. Notice what truths Moses 1 emphasizes. I often wonder how Christianity would be different if this chapter had not been lost.

Spend no more than five minutes thinking about or discussing these questions on your own or with your study group:

- Where's the farthest place you've traveled?

- What culture have you experienced that was the most different from yours?

- What different culture have you experienced that has really impacted you for the better?

- Why do you think it's important to have multicultural experiences?

The vision in Moses 1 is a series of visions and experiences meant to fill Moses with heavenly eyes. Notice how God expanded the vision of Moses to greater and greater heights.

FIRST VISION: MOSES 1:7–8

In the first vision, God showed Moses the earth and "all the children of men which are, and were created." Moses was blown away and spent hours trying to understand what he saw. He concluded that "man is nothing, which thing I never had supposed" (Moses 1:10). Did Moses come to the right conclusion? Is man "nothing"? We know that at the end of this chapter, Moses learned God's work and glory is "to bring to pass the immortality and eternal life of man" (Moses 1:39). God's testimony is that His children are *everything*! This is a "line upon line" revelatory experience. Moses was discovering pieces of truth throughout this entire chapter.

President Dieter F. Uchtdorf explained, "This is a paradox of man: compared to God, man is nothing; yet we are everything to God. While against the backdrop of infinite creation we may appear to be nothing, we have a spark of eternal fire burning within our breast. We have the incomprehensible promise of exaltation—worlds without end—within our grasp. And it is God's great desire to help us reach it."[12]

SECOND VISION: MOSES 1:24–29

In the second portion of this experience, Moses's vision expanded because he was prepared for further light and knowledge. Moses saw every particle of the earth as well as every soul. Verse 29 states, "And he beheld many lands; and each land was called earth, and there were inhabitants on the face thereof." In comparison to verse 8, in the first vision, Moses saw only Egypt and the surrounding areas or "the worlds" with which he was personally familiar. The second vision adds the perspective that God watches over people all over the planet.

At the beginning of this chapter, Moses was taught that he was worth saving (see Moses 1:1–4). He was then taught that all the people he would ever interact with were worth saving (see Moses 1:8). Then he was shown that all of God's children on this earth are worth saving. With this foundation, Moses was prepared for a final vision-stretching experience!

THIRD VISION: MOSES 1:35–38

The Lord then now showed Moses what He has been up to throughout all eternity. Moses was shown "many worlds" like ours "that have passed away by the word of [His] power. And there are many that now stand" (Moses 1:35). God started with the *present,* and then He showed Moses the *past.* In verse 38, Moses was ready for the final phase, which was the *future*: "And as one earth shall pass away . . . so shall another come; and there is no end to my works, neither to my words" (Moses 1:38). Past, present, future! Joseph Smith was taught, "And truth is knowledge of things as they are [*present*], and as they were [*past*], and as they are to come [*future*]."[13] The pattern is the same for Moses, Joseph Smith, and many other prophets and seers in the scriptures.

The Lord showed Moses all of this to prepare him for God's profound and eternally important mission statement: "For behold, this is my work and my glory—to bring to pass the immortality and eternal life of man" (Moses 1:39). Before Moses was used to liberate over one million Hebrews from 400 years of slavery, he needed to understand—and never forget—that *all of God's children are worth saving, past, present, and future!* This is how you start a book of scripture!

---

12 "You Matter to Him," *Ensign* or *Liahona*, November 2011, 20.

13 Doctrine and Covenants 93:24

- What do you think Moses knew after this series of visions that he didn't fully realize before?

- In what ways could this new perspective have been useful to Moses as he was preparing to liberate the children of Israel from Egypt?

- How do you think this perspective caused Moses to mourn at the pharaoh's continual pridefulness?

- Why was it important for the children of Israel to be led by a prophet who is, to some extent, "full of eyes"?

IS JESUS CHRIST WORTH WORSHIPPING? (15 MINUTES)

The Lord taught life-changing truths to Moses, and all of us, in Moses 1:

- Moses is a child of God (see Moses 1:4).

- His life has purpose and meaning (see Moses 1:6).

- What God offers is far greater than what Satan offers (see Moses 1:13–16).

- God wants to connect with His children in deeply personal ways (see Moses 1:1, 11).

- God is with Moses and will never give up on him (see Moses 1:26).

- Moses can always trust in Jesus Christ because of His profound character (see Moses 1:32).

- Because God is full of eyes, He sees all of us individually, we are His, and He knows us (see Moses 1:35).

If you haven't already, take a few minutes to mark each of these truths in Moses 1. Which of these do you have a testimony of? Which of these is harder for you to see right now? Take a few minutes to either write down or share your testimony using the following prompt:

A personal relationship with Jesus Christ is important to me because _____ .

How does the following video by a modern-day "see-er" help us draw personal strengths from the visions of Moses?

Gospel Library app -> Videos -> Inspirational Messages -> Dieter F. Uchtdorf, "Our True Identity"

Or scan the following QR code

(or google "Dieter F. Uchtdorf Our True Identity")

HOW TO SLAY A DRAGON (10 MINUTES)

If you were to fight a dragon and you could only use two weapons, what would you choose?

In Revelation 12:7–11, John the Beloved helps us peek into our premortal life. Yes, he was another "see-er" who was trying to expand our vision. He was clearly reminding us of *how* we overcame Satan (the dragon) there. The two weapons John highlighted were

- the "blood of the lamb"

- "the word of their testimony"[14]

Between the first and second visions Moses had, he experienced the influence of Satan. Although Moses didn't yet see everything, notice how he used the exact same premortal weapons to overcome Satan in mortality.

VISION OF SATAN: MOSES 1:12–22

- The blood of the lamb

- Power of his testimony

The Lord emphasizes a premortal understanding of the plan of salvation in Abraham 3:19–27. How can understanding where we came from give us power and perspective in the present?

Let me conclude with one final thought about the confrontation Moses had with Satan. Many people have spoken to me about the darkness they have felt in their lives. Sometimes this darkness overwhelms them because of poor choices, sometimes it overwhelms them just because, and often it is a combination of the two. Usually, the conversation turns to the person concluding that God must not care much for them, because how can they be a heavenly being and still feel attacked by so much darkness? Remember, Moses felt this darkness;

---

14 Revelation 12:11.

Joseph Smith felt it in the Sacred Grove.[15] Joseph also saw outer darkness in a vision just before being shown the celestial kingdom.[16] Lehi walked through a lone and dreary waste and prayed for hours before he saw the tree of life.[17] Alma the Younger was racked with eternal torment and inexpressible horror just before his redemptive experience.[18] Just because we experience legitimate darkness does not mean God is mad at us, doesn't love us, or has forgotten about us.

To this concern, I would refer you to someone who experienced serious darkness in his life: Abinadi. Just before he was martyred, he testified that Jesus Christ is "the light and the life of the world; yea, a light that is endless, that can never be darkened; yea and also a life which is endless, that there can be no more death."[19] Abinadi understood that Jesus Christ can bring light to all darkness. It makes me wonder what darkness he went through *before* he went to the court of King Noah that prepared him to testify so boldly of Jesus Christ as the light and life of the world.

---

15 Joseph Smith—History 1:15.
16 Doctrine and Covenants 76:31–50.
17 1 Nephi 8:8.
18 Alma 36:14–20.
19 Mosiah 16:9.

JANUARY 3–9
"IN THE BEGINNING GOD CREATED THE HEAVEN AND THE EARTH"
GENESIS 1–2; MOSES 2–3; ABRAHAM 4–5

God's Message to Me from This Section

WHAT IS THE CREATION STORY TRYING TO TEACH US? (15 MINUTES)

Take a few minutes to see if you can brainstorm at least three answers to the question above:

1. _____

_____

2. _____

_____

3. _____

_____

If you do any type of comparison of these Creation stories, you will quickly notice the sequence of events is not consistent. That's okay! The Creation stories will not teach you the science behind God's creative process. That's okay! Why? Because it was *never* meant to answer those questions. The Creation story was not written to answer *how* Heavenly Father and Jesus Christ created the earth; it was written to teach us *why* they did it. Shifting your perspective from "*how creation*" to "*why creation*" will allow this story to speak to you in ways that will testify, like Moses 1, that you are worth saving! It will testify of the first paragraph of the Young Women theme:

"I am a beloved daughter of heavenly parents, with a divine nature and eternal destiny."

As you read about the Creation, consider the following:

- Mark how many times you see the word *God* in Genesis 1 and Moses 2. Why do you think God reminds us repeatedly that He oversaw and participated in the Creation?

- Abraham 4 uses *the Gods* instead of *God*. What additional perspective does this add?

- After each creative period, "it was so," or "God saw that it was good" (Genesis 1:7–12, 18, 21, 24–25). In contrast, when God, or the Gods, created man and then woman, their commentary was, "Behold, it was *very* good" (Genesis 1:31, *emphasis added*). Considering Moses 1:39, what are some possible reasons why the Gods have a unique interest in the creation of humanity?

- In Genesis 2:18, Eve is referred to as "an help meet" for Adam. On the surface, this may seem to diminish Eve's status, and by extension, all of womanhood is seemingly placed below manhood. Before you draw that conclusion, consider this: the Hebrew word for "help meet" is *ezer*.[20] This word is used twenty-one times in the Old Testament, and nineteen of those occurrences use *ezer* in direct reference

---

20 *Bible Hub*, s.v. "ezer," https://biblehub.com/hebrew/5828.htm

to the power of Jehovah to help us. The other two occurrences are used in reference to Eve. In this context, Genesis 2:18 takes on at least one new meaning. "And the Lord God said, It is not good that the man should be alone; I will make him an help meet for him." If Eve represents Jehovah, then Adam represents humanity because it really is not good for mankind to be left without Jehovah, the *Divine Helper*. Maybe a better question is, In what ways is Eve, and all women, a type for Jesus Christ? (Hint: think birth and creation)

- In Genesis 2:24, we get three adjectives that describe what God hoped Adam and Eve would incorporate into their marriage relationship: *leave, cleave, be one*. Jesus quoted this verse during His mortal ministry.[21] Let's focus on the word *cleave*. The Hebrew word for *cleave* used in Genesis 2:24 means "to cling, to keep close, to stay, to join, to be deeply attracted, to remain steadfast."[22] The Greek word used in Matthew 19:5 has a similar meaning but adds, "[literally] glued together, [figuratively] intimately connected in a soul-knit friendship."[23] Similar to Genesis 2:18, if we use Adam as a representative for humanity and Eve as a representative of Christ, how can the Hebrew and Greek definitions of *cleave* describe Jesus's intentions toward us?

- Watch the following video and think about how the Creation itself testifies of the importance of diversity.

(or google "We don't need to be the same to be one")

Go back to the first question: What is the Creation story trying to teach us? After studying, what did the Creation story teach you this week?

In 1996, President Russell M. Nelson expanded our definition of *creation* in these three ways:

- The creation of Adam and Eve was a *paradisiacal creation,* one that required a significant change before they could fulfill the commandment to have children and thus provide earthly bodies for premortal spirit sons and daughters of God.

- The Fall of Adam (and Eve) constituted the *mortal creation* and brought about the required changes in their bodies, including the circulation of blood and other modifications as well.

- The Atonement of Jesus Christ became the *immortal creation.* He volunteered to answer the ends of a law previously transgressed.[24]

BE A KID AGAIN! (10 MINUTES)

If you had asked me when I was eight years old what I wanted to be when I grew up, I would have told you proudly, "A tractor driver!" I would sit in the sandbox in my backyard for hours and hours creating cities, building castles, digging small rivers and lakes. It was all possible because of my tractor toys and because children of God are creators! As children of a Creator, we seek ways to create. We create businesses, art, products, opportunities, services, music, poetry, families, technology, etc. As I look back, my deep desire to create fueled my sandbox joy.

As a kid, what did you want to be when you grew up? If you have little kids, ask them what they want to be. How can you see a desire for creation in these occupations?

What are some things you do now to create?

Chad Webb, administrator of seminaries and institutes of religion, told the following story:

You may remember that President Boyd K. Packer was an accomplished artist who enjoyed carving wooden birds. One day, he was a passenger in a car driven by Elder A. Theodore Tuttle, and one of his carvings rested on the backseat of the car. At an intersection, Elder Tuttle slammed on the brakes and the carving tipped upside down on the floor and broke into pieces. Elder Tuttle was devastated, but President Packer was not. He simply said, "Forget it. I made it. I can fix it." And he did. He made it stronger than it was and even improved it a bit. President Packer explained, "Who made you? Who is

---

21 Matthew 19:5.
22 *Bible Hub*, s.v. "dabaq," https://biblehub.com/hebrew/1692.htm.
23 *Bible Hub* s.v. "kollaó," https://biblehub.com/greek/2853.htm.
24 See "The Atonement," *Ensign*, November 1996, 33–34.

your Creator? There is not anything about your life that gets bent or broken that He cannot fix and will fix."[25]

Because Jesus Christ is our Creator, He knows how to heal us!

As you watch the following video, think about ways the Creation testifies of its Creator.

Gospel Library App -> Videos and Images -> Holiday Videos -> Easter Videos -> Because of Him

(or google "Because of Him Easter Video")

THE CREATION—A LESSON FOR TEACHERS (5 MINUTES)

In answering the question, "How can I provide the best classroom environment for gospel learning?" Neill F. Marriott used principles of the Creation to teach the following:

Can you see how the Lord's creation of the earth is a pattern for your creation of a classroom environment? The Lord, under the direction of His Father, created the divinely designed classroom that we call earth

- By faith,
- By spiritual planning,
- By loving and orderly effort,
- By strict obedience, and
- By knowing what Heavenly Father's children need in order to grow and prosper.

You, too, can follow the Lord's way, in your own limited mortal fashion, to create a spiritually designed place of truth and freedom. Such an act of creation requires holiness of heart. There is nothing halfhearted about creating a holy place of learning.

It's your space. I like to think that in the best classrooms there is really no empty space! From wall to wall and floor to ceiling, it is full of love and acceptance, built on faith in the Savior's Atonement and teachings.[26]

Whether it's a classroom or your home, are there any principles of creation you feel to focus on this week?

---

25 "We Talk of Christ, We Rejoice in Christ," Seminaries and Institutes of Religion Annual Training Broadcast, June 12, 2018, Conference Center Theater. See also, Boyd K. Packer, "The Instrument of Your Mind and the Foundation of Your Character" Church Educational System devotional for young adults, Feb. 2, 2003, 9, speeches.byu.edu.

26 "A Sense of Place," Seminaries and Institutes of Religion Annual Training Broadcast, June 14, 2016.

JANUARY 10–16
THE FALL OF ADAM AND EVE
GENESIS 3–4; MOSES 4–5

God's Message to Me from This Section

WHERE ART THOU? (10 MINUTES)

In my opinion, this is one of the most useful questions in all of scripture. We too often ask ourselves where we want to go without first seeking to understand where we are! Even Google Maps teaches us this principle! If you type in a destination, you will *never* get directions unless you also enter a starting point. Usually, we use our "current location."

When Adam and Eve partook of the fruit, Satan told them to cover up and hide, and they did. A loving Father soon arrived and asked them, "Where art thou?" (Genesis 3:9). As far as I know, God doesn't ask many questions He doesn't already know the answer to. This question was not for Him. God knew where they were. This question was for Adam and Eve to better understand their "current location." Sometimes I wonder how long it took Adam and Eve to come out from hiding.

My invitation for you is to better understand your current location. Where are you regarding your relationship with our Heavenly Parents and Jesus Christ? Where are you in other important aspects of your life? In other words, speak *your* truth just as Adam and Eve spoke theirs so many years ago. Be real, be vulnerable, be willing to come out from hiding, be honest.

The very first words John the Beloved gave Jesus in his gospel was a question. When Peter and his brother Andrew first began to follow Jesus, the Savior asked, "What seek ye?"[27] Considering what you wrote about your "current location," take a few minutes to write about what you seek, or what you want this year as you study the Old Testament.

---

27 John 1:38.

_____

_____

_____

_____

LET'S TALK ELEPHANTS (15 MINUTES)

If you had a pet elephant, what would you build to keep it from running away? What changes would you need to make as your elephant got bigger?

Jack Canfield, the author of *Chicken Soup for the Soul*, explained:

A [captive] baby elephant is trained at birth to be confined to a very small space. Its trainer will tie its leg with a rope to a wooden post planted deep in the ground. This confines the baby elephant to an area determined by the length of the rope. . . . Though the baby elephant will initially try to break the rope, the rope is too strong, and so the baby elephant learns that it can't break the rope. It learns that it has to stay in the area defined by the length of the rope.

When the elephant grows up into a 5–ton colossus that could easily break the same rope, it doesn't even try because it learned as a baby that it couldn't break the rope. In this way, the largest elephant can be confined by the puniest little rope.[28]

This story has always been important to me when I think about the power of believing lies. As mentioned earlier, one of Satan's oldest lies is that when we feel fear, we need to cover up and hide (see Genesis 3:7–8,10). From my own experience, let me assure you that covering up

and hiding is the *worst* way to manage difficulties in life! I've found nothing but pain in hiding my vulnerabilities from God and others who want to help me.

Notice how a loving God mentors His children. He identifies the liar, Satan. God assures Adam and Eve that His own voice has never and will never speak those lies. Then He provides His fearful children with a beautiful object lesson. Embedded in this object lesson is the *truth* to combat the *lie*. Genesis 3:21 teaches, "Unto Adam also and to his wife did the Lord God make coats of skins, and clothed them." When Adam and Eve get dressed each day, they are wrapped in clothing. Lehi best taught the feelings attached to this action when he testified, "But behold, the Lord hath redeemed my soul from hell; I have beheld his glory, and I am encircled about eternally in the arms of his love."[29] The *truth* that will motivate all of us to come out from hiding is that *we are worth saving*! Adam and Eve were given a daily reminder, through clothing, so they would never forget their worth and their eternal potential. If they always remember this truth, it will be much more difficult for them to believe the lie that they should cover up and hide—because they are already covered in Christ, and Christ sees them and knows them no matter their current location.

Here is a simple way to know where the voices you are listening to come from. This is meant to be observed without judgment. If you struggle with this, it may be because Satan is really good at telling this particular lie. He has been doing it for thousands of years! You and I have been on Earth for about ten minutes, so don't beat yourself up.

Satan will tell you . . .	God will tell you . . .
I am a mistake.	You made a mistake.
I am bad.	You did something bad.
I should give up.	Let's do this together.
I am alone.	I am always with you.
I am worthless.	You are worth saving.

Notice Satan will always attack your identity. God will never do that because your identity is a cosmic constant. It never changes no matter what you do. If you need further proof, I submit to you Alma the Younger and the Prodigal Son.

_____

28 Jack Canfield, "The Success Principles," 71.

29 2 Nephi 1:15.

Maybe now is a good time to watch this video by J. Devn Cornish, of the Seventy. He does an incredible job teaching what I view as the most important principles we can learn from the Fall.

(or google "Am I Good Enough J Devn Cornish")

"TOO MANY RULES AND NOT ENOUGH SINNING" (15 MINUTES)

One hot, humid afternoon, my missionary companion and I were knocking on doors in Detroit, Michigan, looking for people to teach. After we knocked on one particular door, it flew open, and a rather enthusiastic guy in his early twenties greeted us with a huge smile. Caught off guard, we asked if he knew who we were. He explained that he had recently broken up with a girl who was a member of The Church of Jesus Christ of Latter-day Saints. They had been dating for almost a year. We quickly shifted the conversation to what he thought of attending church and young single adult activities. He laughed about how there always seemed to be a lot of food and a lot of prayers at every Church event. Near the end of our conversation, he said something I will never forget: "I can sum up your church in one sentence: there are too many rules and not enough sinning!" We left him with a Book of Mormon and never heard from him again.

Have you ever felt that in our Church, there are too many rules and not enough sinning? I have. In fact, this experience has completely redefined why I live the commandments. Let's begin with where this philosophy came from. In Genesis 3:1, we are introduced to a serpent that is "more subtil than any beast of the field." Notice this subtlety in his interaction with Eve. As they are in the garden looking around at all the many trees, the serpent asks, "Yea, hath God said, Ye shall not eat of every tree of the garden?" Let me take some liberty and reword what I think he is really asking: "Because God loves you so much, he will let you eat of *every* tree in the garden, right?" The subtlety here is interesting. Satan wanted to put God's love and God's laws in competition rather than companionship with each other. Satan also shifted Eve's perspective. She was no longer considering all the trees she *could* partake of; she was focused only on the one tree she *couldn't* partake of (see Genesis 3:1–3). (To be clear, we know Eve and Adam's decision to partake of the fruit of the tree of knowledge of good and evil was *not* a sin but a transgression.)

Isn't Satan's subtle reframe of commandments essentially the same as saying, "There are too many rules and not enough sinning"? Satan would have us hyperfocus on what we *can't do*, so we are blinded to all of the things we *can do*. Another manifestation of this focus is when we focus too much on what we *are not*; when we look in the mirror, we no longer recognize all the amazing things we *are*. Therefore, comparison is not a useful mindset because we believe the lie that we are never enough, we are inherently broken, and we are beyond repair. When I have believed these lies, I have observed an increase in bitterness and resentment toward God. I get trapped in the mindset of noticing only all the things I don't have and I find it's hard to feel joy in what I do have. Let me conclude this thought with one warning: please do not take this too far and pretend like there's nothing wrong at all. My point is to recognize the lie so we can manage it in more useful ways.

How can we combat these lies? The scriptures even tell us to "live in thanksgiving daily" (Alma 34:38). How can we do that? For me, keeping a gratitude journal has been incredibly helpful. You can do this in many ways. Every night, before I go to bed, I take a few minutes to write three things I am grateful for that day and one thing I learned. I can testify from my own experience that what Elder Dieter F. Uchtdorf taught is true:

> Those who set aside the bottle of bitterness and lift instead the goblet of gratitude can find a purifying drink of healing, peace, and understanding. . . .
>
> All of His commandments are given to make blessings available to us. Commandments are opportunities to exercise our agency and to receive blessings. . . .
>
> Being grateful in times of distress does *not* mean that we are pleased with our circumstances. It *does* mean that through the eyes of faith we look beyond our present-day challenges.

This is not a gratitude of the lips but of the soul. It is a gratitude that heals the heart and expands the mind. . . .

Gratitude is a catalyst to all Christlike attributes! A thankful heart is the parent of all virtues.[30]

TESTIMONIES OF WOMEN IN SCRIPTURE (10 MINUTES)

For whatever reason, we do not get nearly as many testimonies from women as we do from men in the scriptures. Along with Eve's testimony, here are a few others you may want to read and analyze. What do these women know about the character of Christ? What perspective do they have because of their painful experiences? How can their testimonies bring you hope when you feel like God doesn't notice you?

- Eve's testimony (see Moses 5:11)

- Hannah's testimony (see 1 Samuel 2:1–10)

- Mary's testimony (see Luke 1:46–55)

- Sariah's testimony (see 1 Nephi 5:7–8)

APPROACHING CAIN AND ABEL WITHOUT JUDGMENT (5 MINUTES)

Much of Moses 5 focuses on Cain and Abel, two men who often symbolize all that is bad and all that is good. When members of The Church of Jesus Christ of Latter-day Saints think of Cain and Abel, they should also consider Laman and Nephi. Unfortunately, it is easy to read these stories and think about all the people we know who might be more like Cain and Laman. Too often, we label these people as all bad, which is rarely, if ever, the case. We are tempted to think in terms of "us versus them," "Christians versus atheists," "men versus women," "race versus race," "Republicans versus Democrats." Please resist this temptation! Rather, think of Cain and Abel as extremes on a continuum that live inside of *you*. On one side, you have Cain and what he represents; on the other side, you have Abel and what he represents. The same would go for Laman and Nephi. Then ask yourself how you are doing regarding your most important relationships. Do you lean more toward Cain or more toward Abel? How can you be a little more like Nephi today and a little less like Laman?

---

30 "Grateful in Any Circumstances," *Ensign*, May 2014, 75–77.

JANUARY 17–23
"TEACH THESE THINGS FREELY UNTO YOUR CHILDREN"
GENESIS 5; MOSES 6

God's Message to Me from This Section

ENOCH'S STORY, MY STORY (15 MINUTES)

What are some of the ways you have experienced the Fall? Your list may include depression, disability, divorce, abuse, war, trauma, disease. What else would you add? How have some of these experiences brought feelings of hopelessness? Sometimes I look to God and say, "I see the wisdom in experiencing the Fall, but did we really have to fall *this* far?"

President Russell M. Nelson told a story about the Fall that has stuck with me for 20 years:

> While visiting the British Museum in London one day, I read a most unusual book. It is not scripture. It is an English translation of an ancient Egyptian manuscript. From it, I quote a dialogue between the Father and the Son. Referring to His Father, Jehovah—the premortal Lord—says:
>
> "He took the clay from the hand of the angel, and made Adam according to Our image and likeness, and He left him lying for forty days and forty nights without putting breath into him. And He heaved sighs over him daily, saying, 'If I put breath into this [man], he must

suffer many pains.' And I said unto My Father, 'Put breath into him; I will be an advocate for him.' And My Father said unto Me, 'If I put breath into him, My beloved Son, Thou wilt be obliged to go down into the world, and to suffer many pains for him before Thou shalt have redeemed him, and made him to come back to his primal state.' And I said unto My Father, 'Put breath into him; I will be his advocate, and I will go down into the world, and will fulfil Thy command.'"

> Although this text is not scripture, it reaffirms scriptures that teach of the deep and compassionate love of the Father for the Son, and of the Son for us—attesting that Jesus volunteered willingly to be our Savior and Redeemer.[31]

Enoch, like many others in scripture, experienced the Fall in difficult ways. An interesting exercise to work through is to tell the story of the same person through two very different perspectives. Here's a simple example of how you could do this with Enoch:

---

31 "The Creation," *Ensign* or *Liahona*, May 2000, 84.

Enoch's failures and hardships . . .	Enoch's triumphs and transcendence . . .
"I am slow of speech" (Moses 6:31)	"So powerful was the word of Enoch (Moses 7:13)
"All the people hate me" (Moses 6:31)	"He walked with God" (Moses 6:34, 39; Genesis 5:22, 24)
"All men were offended because of him" (Moses 6:37)	He built a unified city of Zion, where people were of "one heart and one mind . . . and there was no poor among them" (Moses 7:18)

All the above is part of Enoch's story. Like Enoch, our lives are marked by contradictions and paradoxes that can be extremely difficult to reconcile. Let's try this together. Below, brainstorm how your life has followed Enoch's pattern and so many others.

My failures and hardships . . .	My triumphs and transcendence . . .

SELF-REFLECTION QUESTIONS:

- Are there any other scriptural examples of people who have experienced the extremes of the Fall? (Nephi, Alma the Younger, Moses, Mary the mother of Jesus, etc.)
- What are some possible reasons that God uses such dramatic stories in the scriptures?

- In what ways are you more like Jesus Christ because of the difficult experiences you've faced?
- In what ways did Jesus Himself experience the extreme highs and lows of the Fall?
- Because of the Fall, God wants me to understand
  _____.

HOW DO I RECONCILE THE PARADOXES OF LIFE? (15 MINUTES)

Now that we've identified how the Fall impacts our mortal experiences—in other words, the Fall *is* our mortal experience—let's look at how Enoch can help us work through these difficulties in more heavenly ways.

President Ezra Taft Benson taught the following beautiful connection between the Atonement and the Fall: "Just as a man does not really desire food until he is hungry, so he does not desire the salvation of Christ until he knows why he needs Christ. No one adequately and properly knows why he needs Christ until he understands and accepts the doctrine of the Fall and its effect upon all mankind."[32]

As you study the following scriptures from Moses 6, see if you can identify how Enoch allowed the Atonement of Jesus Christ to help him through his difficulties:

- Moses 6:31–33 _____
- Moses 6:42–43 _____
- Moses 6:51–52 _____
- Moses 6:55 _____

How does experiencing the extremes of mortality allow space for the Holy Ghost to be more involved in your life? Can you think of an experience where you felt the light of the Holy Ghost at a time of extreme darkness?

Look for examples of opposite words in the following video. After the video, discuss how this person's experience is a useful lesson for our own difficulties in mortality.

Gospel Library -> Videos and Images -> Inspirational Videos -> Your Great Adventure: Overcoming Life's Obstacles

---

32 *A Witness and a Warning*, (Salt Lake City: Deseret Book, 1988), 33.

(or google "Your Great Adventure: Overcoming Life's Obstacles")

TEACHING JOY IN THE CONTEXT OF PAIN (10 MINUTES)

In the Book of Mormon, Jacob's son Enos is a fascinating example of the application of what Enoch taught. Read Moses 6:57–62. Now read Enos 1:3–4 and notice what motivated Enos to personally seek Jesus Christ. What created Enoch's hunger?

> "Behold, I went to hunt beasts in the forests; and the words which I had often heard my father speak concerning eternal life, and the joy of the saints, sunk deep into my heart. And my soul hungered."[33]

Jacob taught his son perspective (eternal life) and the joy of the Saints. Interesting. My assumption early on in life was that the joy of the Saints was Jacob showing Enos that when you live the gospel, life gets much easier and, therefore, more joyful. I have since learned that was a very false assumption. The culture Jacob and his family were in was *not* a joyful paradise where no bad things happened because they were faithful. The book of Jacob is full of wounded and broken hearts,[34] grieving souls,[35] great anxiety,[36] destructive pride,[37] every kind of sin,[38] and an anti-Christ.[39] How did Jacob then talk in such a motivating way about "the joy of the saints"? I believe that, like Enoch, Jacob taught heavenly joy through the context of mortal pain. Teaching joy without pain is *not* joy. We learn the value of peace through experiencing pain. We learn the value of resurrection through experiencing the death of someone close to us. We learn the

value of light through experiencing darkness. In Moses 6:58, Enoch invited his people "to teach these things freely unto your children." Moses 6:59–62 is specifically the joy that can be found in the pain of life. Here are some of the descriptions I noticed:

- Moses 6:59—Rebirth through the water, blood, and spirit (intimate personal relationship with Jesus Christ)
- Moses 6:59—Sanctification from all sin (becoming like Christ)
- Moses 6:59—En*joy* the words of eternal life in *this world*
- Moses 6:59—Eternal life in the world to come
- Moses 6:61—The Comforter
- Moses 6:61—The peaceable things of immortal glory
- Moses 6:61—The truth of all things
- Moses 6:61—Life, knowledge, and power
- Moses 6:62—The plan of salvation!

What are some ways we can teach our children and others joy through the context of pain? What role does vulnerability play in these discussions? Who is a good example to you of someone who teaches joy using the context of pain? Can you think of an example of how President Nelson has taught in this way?

Gospel Library -> Videos and Images -> Inspirational Videos -> Hear Him to Find Peace During Turbulent Times

(or google "Hear Him to Find Peace During Turbulent Times President Nelson")

---

33 Enos 1:3–4.
34 See Jacob 2:35.
35 See Jacob 2:6.
36 See Jacob 1:5.
37 See Jacob 2:16.
38 See Jacob 3:12.
39 See Jacob 7:2.

JANUARY 24–30
"THE LORD CALLED HIS PEOPLE ZION"
MOSES 7

God's Message to Me from This Section

SPIRITUAL EXPERIENCES IN MOVIES (15 MINUTES)

Have you ever had a true spiritual experience while watching a movie? I have! It is one of my favorite experiences. Near the end of the epic Marvel movie *Thor: Ragnarok* (2017), the survivors of a place named Asgard watch in devastation as their city is destroyed. Asgard is a complicated city in Marvel comics but generally teaches that the peace the people choose to live in allows them to experience love and unity. It is an interesting comic representation of what the scriptures call Zion. Immediately after Asgard is destroyed, Thor cries out, "What have I done?" Full of wisdom, an Asgardian seer named Heimdall responds, "Asgard is not a place; it's a people." In the theater, I remember responding in a hushed whisper, "Whoa! That's a Zion principle!" Don't judge me.

See if you can come up with three to five movies, or movie quotes, that teach spiritual lessons.

1. _____

2. _____

3. _____

4. _____

5. _____

It may come as a shock that it took Enoch about 365 years to build Zion to a point where it was prepared to be translated and taken into heaven.[40] Most of us assume he did it in less than 100 years. By comparison, the United States of America isn't even 250 years old.

Read the following scriptural descriptions of Zion. Specifically notice the characteristics of the people and the relationship they have with God and each other.

Moses 7:3–4 _____

Moses 7:13 _____

Moses 7:16–23 _____

Moses 7:56 _____

Moses 7:69 _____

---

40 *Teachings of the Presidents of the Church: Brigham Young* (1997), 94; see also Genesis 5:21–24; Moses 7:68–69; 8:1; D&C 107:48–49.

Doctrine and Covenants 97:21 _____

Doctrine and Covenants 24:7 _____

Doctrine and Covenants 136:31 _____

4 Nephi 1:15–18 _____

What are some additional ways you would describe Zion-like people?

Look at the descriptions of a Zion people above and choose one of them to incorporate into your home this week. Circle it and pray to receive God's help in your adventure.

A GOD WHO WEEPS (15 MINUTES)

Out of all the visions in the scriptures, which ones are the most impactful to you personally?

- Lehi's vision of the tree of life (see 1 Nephi 8)

- Moses's vision of Jesus Christ and all His creations (see Moses 1)

- Joseph Smith's First Vision (see JS—H 1:16–17)

- Joseph Smith's vision of the kingdoms of glory (see Doctrine and Covenants 76)

- Isaiah's vision of Jesus Christ (see Isaiah 6)

- Nephi's vision of the ministry and Atonement of Jesus Christ (see 1 Nephi 11–14)

- Joseph's vision of Jesus, Moses, Elias, and Elijah in the Kirtland Temple (see Doctrine and Covenants 110)

- The Brother of Jared's vision of Christ's spirit body (see Ether 3)

- Alma the Younger's vision of the angel who calls him to repentance (see Alma 36)

- King Lamoni's vision of the Redeemer (see Alma 19:6, 12–13)

- Others: _____

Choose one of the visions above and write some possible characteristics of Jesus Christ that the person (or people) learned from these experiences. In other words, what did they know about Jesus *after* these experiences that they may not have fully understood *before*?

As Moses experienced in Moses 1, Enoch experienced both Christ's light and life along with Satan's depth of evil and darkness. As you read Moses 7:24–33, identify all the characteristics of Satan as well as the characteristics of Christ.

I can't read this without thinking of Jesus interacting with Mary and Martha four days after their brother, and Jesus's friend, Lazarus, died. It is safe to assume that Jesus knew He would raise Lazarus from the dead. In fact, it seems from the scriptures that He intentionally waited to go to Mary and Martha to help them.[41] Even with Christ's surprisingly late arrival, Martha testified, "Lord, if thou hadst been here, my brother had not died. But I know, that even now, whatsoever thou wilt ask of God, God will give it thee."[42] We receive the shortest and maybe most profound verse in all of scripture as Jesus walked with Mary and Martha. Even knowing what He could and would do, Jesus did not dismiss the grief of Mary and Martha, rather, "Jesus wept."[43]

We learn from scripture that we worship a God who weeps! Enoch is shocked by this revelation. How can Jesus, with perfect character, weep? Isn't He above shedding tears? It appears He sheds both blood and tears because of His deep connection with each of us. Can you think of experiences where you think Jesus has wept with you? What does it mean to you to know that Jesus weeps with us in our grief and pain?

The next time grief, pain, or loss lead you to weep, please know your tears are not evidence of mortal weakness. Rather, each tear is evidence of your divine strength! You need never apologize for divine tears.

IS THIS A DESCRIPTION OF GETHSEMANE AND CALVARY? (5 MINUTES)

Moses 7:41 speaks of Enoch and the Lord. I'm going to rewrite this verse as a potential interaction between the Father and the Son during Gethsemane and the Crucifixion: "And it came to pass that Heavenly Father spake unto Jesus, and told Jesus all the doings of the children of men; wherefore Jesus knew, and looked upon their wickedness, and their misery, and wept and stretched forth His arms, and His heart swelled wide as eternity; and His bowels yearned; and all eternity shook."

---

41 See John 11:6, 17, 39.
42 John 11:21–22.
43 John 11:35.

If the brokenness Jesus experienced in Gethsemane and on Calvary caused His heart to swell "wide as eternity," wouldn't that explain His infinite supply of compassion? Wouldn't that explain why He will never give up on us? Is this part of what the scriptures refer to when they testify that Jesus is "full of grace and truth"?[44]

A companion verse in Doctrine and Covenants 88:6 has a similar, albeit less poetic, tone as Moses 7:41: "He that ascended up on high, as also he descended below all things, in that he comprehended all things, that he might be in all and through all things, the light of truth."

Because Jesus Christ chose to be broken and torn apart, He comprehends us completely and His heart swells as wide as eternity. There is nothing in my life or yours that is outside of His compassionate gaze!

---

44 See Doctrine and Covenants 93:11; 2 Nephi 2:6.

JANUARY 31–FEBRUARY 6
"NOAH FOUND GRACE IN THE EYES OF THE LORD"
GENESIS 6–11; MOSES 8

God's Message to Me from This Section

Noah was called to preach the gospel 120 years before the flood, which, according to many Bible scholars, happened between 2400 BC and 2300 BC. Noah was Enoch's great-grandson and was ordained to the higher priesthood by his grandfather Methuselah when he was ten years old.[45] And though Noah was not alive at the time the city of Enoch was translated, he was charged in his lifetime with teaching the people who did not, and would not, choose to live in Zion. Noah had a tough calling!

THE FLOOD TESTIFIES OF CHRIST (5 MINUTES)

In the Book of Mormon, Jacob gave us significant observations regarding why many Jews "stumbled":

> But behold, the Jews were a stiffnecked people; and they despised the words of plainness, and killed the prophets, and sought for things that they could not understand. Wherefore, because of their blindness, *which blindness came by looking beyond the mark, they must needs fall*; for God hath taken away his plainness from them, and delivered unto them many things which they cannot

understand, because they desired it. And because they desired it God hath done it, that they may stumble.[46]

Sometimes I wonder if the mark Jacob referred to is one of the marks graven in the palms of Jesus's hands, feet, and side. This observation takes on a much deeper meaning when participating in a temple endowment session.

In my experience, the story of Noah is one of the best biblical examples we have of "looking beyond the mark." For example, we obsess over questions like, Where is the ark? The ark wasn't big enough for two of *every* animal to fit; how do we explain that? How did it rain enough to flood the earth? Is there any scientific evidence of a flood? As you read this story, I am not telling you that these questions aren't valid; I am simply inviting you to focus on the *point* rather than the *periphery* of this story. In other words, please don't look beyond the [m]ark! (See what I did there?)

All of these questions have some validity but only in context of the *entire* story. As you begin this week's study, don't get so focused on certain details that you look "beyond the mark." In these chapters, look for elements of the mission, ordinances, and Atonement of Jesus

---

45 Doctrine and Covenants 107:52.

46 Jacob 4:14, *emphasis added.*

Christ. Here are some examples:

- "Noah found grace in the eyes of the Lord" (Genesis 6:8). Jesus Christ found grace in the eyes of the Father (Matthew 3:17; 3 Nephi 11:10–11).

- The word *ark* in Hebrew means "box" or "chest." This is the same Hebrew word used to describe the watertight basket that saved baby Moses. This could also foreshadow the Jaredite barges that "were tight like unto a dish." The strength of Noah's ark, baby Moses's ark, and the Jaredite barges will save us (see Genesis 6:13–14; Exodus 2:3; Ether 2:17; 6:7). It is also interesting to note that Moses's mother's willing sacrifice saved him. Likewise, Jesus Christ is our salvation because of *both* our Heavenly Parents' willing sacrifice.

- The Lord planned and specifically designed the ark to save the people from death (see Genesis 6:14–15). The Lord planned and specifically designed the plan of salvation to save us from death (see Mosiah 16:8–9).

- The ark is a place of safety (Genesis 6:17). Jesus Christ is a place of safety (see Helaman 5:12; Alma 34:16).

As you continue reading, see if you can find other aspects of Noah's story that point you to Jesus Christ.

IS DEATH THE WORST THING THAT CAN HAPPEN TO A PERSON? (15 MINUTES)

This question sounds depressing, and maybe it is, but is death the worst thing that can happen to a person? In my observation the answer is a definitive no! Reframing our perspective of death, President Dieter F. Uchtdorf taught, "The more we learn about the gospel of Jesus Christ, the more we realize that endings here in mortality are not endings at all. They are merely interruptions—temporary pauses that one day will seem small compared to the eternal joy awaiting the faithful. How grateful I am to my Heavenly Father that in His plan there are no true endings, only everlasting beginnings."[47]

The story of the flood may be more devastating than it is hopeful, just as death feels more devastating than hopeful. In stark contrast to the sadness of the flood story, Nephi taught that Jesus "doeth not anything save it be for the benefit of the world; for he loveth the world, even that he layeth down his own life that he may draw all men unto him."[48] But Noah is told by the same loving Lord, "And, behold, I, even I, do bring a flood of waters upon the earth, to destroy all flesh, wherein is the breath of life, from under heaven; and everything that is in the earth shall die" (Genesis 6:17). How do we reconcile these contradictory verses? Let me share with you a few perspectives that have helped me. Circle the portions below that are useful for you.

A FLOOD FOR THE CHILDREN?

Read what the adults in Noah's time were like in Genesis 6:5 and Moses 8:22. Elder Neal A. Maxwell explained that God intervened "when corruption had reached an agency-destroying point that spirits could not, in justice, be sent here."[49]

President John Taylor explained that "by taking away their earthly existence [God] prevented them from entailing their sins upon their posterity and degenerating [or corrupting] them, and also prevented them from committing further acts of wickedness."[50]

According to these statements, could the flood be beneficial for God's children and future generations?

BOTH SIDES OF THE VEIL

The Apostle Peter taught about hope through the redemption of the dead: "For for this cause was the gospel preached also to them that are dead, that they might be judged according to men in the flesh, but live according to God in the spirit."[51] Because temples gather Israel on *both* sides of the veil, hope and redemption are offered on *both* sides of the veil!

In fact, Peter used the people killed during the flood as evidence of this hope: "By which also [Jesus] went and preached unto the spirits in prison; Which sometime were disobedient, when once the longsuffering of God waited in the days of Noah, while the ark was a preparing, wherein few, that is, eight souls were saved by water."[52]

Similarly, the prophet Joseph F. Smith's life was

47 "Grateful in Any Circumstances," *Ensign*, May 2014, 77.

48 2 Nephi 26:24.
49 "We Will Prove Them Herewith" (1982), 58.
50 "Discourse Delivered by Pres. John Taylor," *Deseret News*, January 16, 1878, 787.
51 1 Peter 4:6.
52 1 Peter 3:19–20.

surrounded by death on a global and personal level.[53] One month before he died at the age of eighty, President Smith had a vision of the redemption of the dead that has since been canonized in the Doctrine and Covenants as section 138. Importantly, he was shown redemption being offered to three general groups of people in the spirit world. See if the wicked people of Noah fit into any of these hope-giving groups:[54]

1. "Those who had died in their sins"

2. "Those who had died . . . without a knowledge of the truth"

3. "Those who had died . . . having rejected the prophets"

Watch the following video as you think about how a greater understanding of the plan of salvation, on both sides of the veil, proves our Savior's love.

(or google "Evie Clair I feel My Savior's Love")

How can this perspective bring you hope when friends and family members are not currently choosing the gospel of Jesus Christ?

"THIS IS ALL GREAT, BUT SERIOUSLY, WHERE IS NOAH'S ARK?" (15 MINUTES)

Now that we've addressed the *mark* (Jesus), let's shift our attention to the location of the *ark*. I know the answer to this question! Are you ready for the big reveal? Noah's ark is the temple! We have saving arks dotting the earth. The purpose of Noah's ark was to save individuals and families from the flood through Christ. The purpose of the temple is to save individuals and families from the Fall through Christ. Here are some other similarities between Noah's ark and modern-day temples:

Noah was a prophet whom God commanded to build an ark with specific instructions.	Joseph Smith was a prophet God commanded to build temples with specific instructions.[55]
Noah built the ark 120 years before the flood in preparation for the destruction.	Joseph Smith, and all subsequent prophets, have been building temples in preparation for the destruction of the Second Coming of Christ.
Noah spent years trying to gather whoever would hear God's voice.	Modern prophets have the charge to gather Israel throughout the world—those who will hear God's voice.[56]
	Doing temple work for our ancestors is extending the same invitation to them as Noah's invitation for his people to join him on the ark.[57]

Scan the following QR code.

(or go to churchofjesuschrist.org/temples)

If you have small children, you may want to have them draw Noah's ark and a temple while you do the following activity:

• Once on this website, click "Find Nearest Temple."

• The nearest temple to you will appear. Click on it.

• On your temple's web page, look for the link that will take you to the dedicatory prayer. It is usually at the bottom.

• Read the dedicatory prayer, and circle any

---

53 M. Russell Ballard, "The Vision of the Redemption of the Dead," *Ensign*, November 2018, 71–73.
54 Doctrine and Covenants 138:32.
55 See *Saints,* vol. 1 (2018), 169.
56 See Doctrine and Covenants 45:56–57; JS-Matt 1:36–37; John 10:3–5,27.
57 See Doctrine and Covenants 138:32–35.

consistencies between Noah's ark and the purpose of your temple.

If you want to explore the location of all the arks (or temples) around the world, scan this QR code. It's a cool feature Google Maps provides.

P.S. Who are the "giants" mentioned in Genesis 6:4? Hebrew Bible scholar Robert Alter explained, "The only obvious meaning of this Hebrew term is 'fallen ones.'"58

P.P.S. My favorite footnote in all of scripture is in Genesis 6:16 regarding what is meant by a "window" in the ark. Genesis 16:6 footnote *a* states, "HEB *tsohar*; some rabbis believed it was a precious stone that shone in the ark. Ether 2:23 (23–24)." It makes you wonder where the Brother of Jared discovered the idea to have Jehovah touch stones to bring light into the barges. This is especially interesting when you consider the flood happened only about 100 years before the Tower of Babel. The Brother of Jared would have been very aware of the details of Noah, the flood, and the ark.

---

58 *The Hebrew Bible: Vol. 1, The Five Books of Moses* (New York: W.W. Norton Co., 2019), 25.

FEBRUARY 7–13
"TO BE A GREATER FOLLOWER OF RIGHTEOUSNESS"
GENESIS 12–17; ABRAHAM 1–2

God's Message to Me from This Section

DIVINE DISPLACEMENT (15 MINUTES)

A few years ago, my little family found ourselves living on the other side of the country. We were jobless, moneyless, and directionless. During this time, we had a birthday party at my house for my wife. Among others, our bishop and a member of the stake presidency came with their families to celebrate with us. They were both good friends of our family. As they began talking to me about what we were going to do, I honestly told them the reality of our situation. After listening intently, my bishop asked, "Has either of you received a blessing?" "No," I replied, a little embarrassed. After the party, they stayed to give us each a blessing. In my blessing, I was told to study the book of Abraham to look for direction. I thought that was just strange enough to be interesting, so I tried it.

The next morning, I sat at the kitchen table with a notepad, colored pencils, and my scriptures. I was ready to deep-dive into Abraham. Where would my direction come from? What would it be? How many times would I have to read the book of Abraham to find answers and direction? I prayed with as much energy and intent as I could, pleading with the Lord to help me find something, anything, that would help us. Then, the search began.

The first verse in Abraham says, "I, Abraham, saw that it was needful for me to obtain another place of residence." As I read this verse, "it seemed to enter with great force into every feeling of my heart."[59] Yes! My answer came in the very first verse of the very first chapter. As I read this verse, the Holy Spirit whispered to me, "It's time for your family to move back across the country." After three months of planning, we moved from the East Coast of Florida to the West Coast of Southern California. Through a series of small, miraculous events over the next two years, and a lot of hard work, I finally received my dream job to be a seminary teacher! In Florida, we never thought that was a possibility. Additionally, my wife's career was greatly enhanced because of this move, and many new opportunities opened for my entire family. As we look back on those experiences, my family praises God for His mercy. I am forever grateful to the book of Abraham and the guidance we received during one of our "wilderness experiences."

Search your memories for a time when a scripture or scripture story answered a prayer for you. If Joseph Smith were in your family, he would excitedly blurt out, "James 1:5!" Scripture stories may include the two thousand stripling warriors, Nephi in the wilderness, the

---

59 See JS—H 1:12.

Crucifixion of Jesus Christ, or His Resurrection. Take a minute to see what you can come up with.

Being displaced is a very common scriptural theme. Wilderness experiences are everywhere in scriptures. Read Abraham 1:2 and look for some important purposes of divine displacement. Mark what Abraham was seeking as he stepped into the dark, not knowing what was in his future.

Have you ever been divinely displaced? In other words, has God ever led you through something terribly difficult? This could be a move, a relationship, a calling, a job change, a new school, an emotional shift, etc.

As you look back on your experience, meditate on the following questions:

- What additional "happiness and peace and rest" did you discover?

- What additional knowledge or perspective do you possess now that you didn't have before?

- Has your confidence in the Lord increased? In what ways?

- Are you still in the darkness? If so, what do you hope to receive from the Lord as you move forward?

- In what ways has priesthood power been useful for you?

SAME FAITH, DIFFERENT OUTCOMES (10 MINUTES)

Elder Dale G. Renlund gave a talk titled "Infuriating Unfairness."[60] He shared,

> A decade ago, while visiting Rwanda, my wife and I struck up a conversation with another passenger at the Kigali airport. He lamented the unfairness of the genocide and poignantly asked, "If there were a God, wouldn't He have done something about it?" For this man—and for many of us—suffering and brutal unfairness can seem incompatible with the reality of a kind, loving Heavenly Father. Yet He is real, He is kind, and He loves each of His children perfectly. This dichotomy is as old as mankind and

cannot be explained in a simple sound bite or on a bumper sticker.

Is "this dichotomy as old as mankind"? We rightly focus on the outcome of Abraham's faith—God led him to a new land, he was very wealthy, and he became the father of many nations. His trials and struggles are also well documented. It is interesting to note that Abraham did highlight "infuriating unfairness" in Abraham 1.

In this chapter, the faithful Abraham found himself tied up and prepared to be sacrificed by the priest of Elkanah. Read Abraham 1:15–20 and notice the outcomes of Abraham's faith. Could you imagine if Abraham were asked to speak to the youth in your stake and he shared this story? We would "stand all amazed at the love Jesus offers [Abraham]!"

But what if Abraham had had the same faith but the outcome had been different? If you go back a few verses, you will read a story of "three virgins" who found themselves in the exact same sacrificial situation as Abraham. I've always wondered if Abraham knew them. "These virgins were offered up [sacrificed] because of their virtue" (see Abraham 1:11). Why didn't the angels loosen *their* bands? Why didn't the Lord deliver *them*? Why didn't the Lord lead *them* by the hand? Abraham experienced all these miracles, so why didn't they?

The scriptures have many similar examples, such as the three Hebrews who were saved from King Nebuchadnezzar's fiery furnace, while King Noah caused Abinadi to suffer "the pains of death by fire."[61]

Elder Renlund continued: "Some unfairness cannot be explained; inexplicable unfairness is infuriating. Unfairness comes from living with bodies that are imperfect, injured, or diseased. Mortal life is inherently unfair. Some people are born in affluence; others are not. Some have loving parents; others do not. Some live many years; others, few. And on and on and on. Some individuals make injurious mistakes even when they are trying to do good. Some choose not to alleviate unfairness when they could. Distressingly, some individuals use their God-given agency to hurt others when they never should."

Take a few minutes to discuss or journal how we can find a loving God as we experience infuriating unfairness. What do you know about the plan of salvation that

---

60 *Liahona*, May 2021.

61 See Daniel 3:25; Mosiah 17:13–15.

could help your perspective during these experiences? Why do you think the Lord is more interested in our faithful offerings than He is in our mortal outcomes?

Elder Renlund concluded by emphasizing the need for perspective and increased faith in the Savior's promise to resolve all unfairness. This can be very difficult at times because we are in the mortal part of the plan where we rarely experience eternal resolution of mortal unfairness. Please do not underestimate the powerful witness the Holy Spirit can bring to console us. For example, during a time when many Nephite women and children were experiencing infuriating unfairness, Jacob taught, "Look unto God with firmness of mind, and pray unto him with exceeding faith, and he will console you in your afflictions, and he will plead your cause, and send down justice upon those who seek your destruction."[62] Interestingly, Jacob did not specify *when* God would send down justice, but he did testify that God *would*.

Knowing the injustices the Apostles would face after His ascension into heaven, Jesus similarly promised, "These things I have spoken unto you, that in me ye might have peace. In the world ye shall have tribulation: but be of good cheer; I have overcome the world."[63]

In the box below, write your personal testimony of Jesus Christ. If you are in a group, please share these testimonies together.

IS IT WORTH IT? (15 MINUTES)

Let's measure some things! If you have small kids, get a tape measure and go around your house and measure things. How tall is your fridge? How wide is your bed? How long is your car or bicycle? You can even measure how tall your kids are and record their height here (if you have grandkids, get their height and write it down). You can compare their height this week to how tall they are at the end of the year.

In Abraham 2:9, the Lord promised Abraham, "I will bless thee above measure." Read Abraham 2:9–12 and mark all of the blessings the Lord promised Abraham. What are some of the ways the Lord has blessed you beyond measure?

Abraham 2 and Genesis 13–17 explain the core of the covenant relationship between God and His children. We call this the Abrahamic Covenant. It is renewed as we make and keep sacred covenants at baptism and in the temple. Covenants are inherently relational. They are eternally expansive, meaning they transcend mortality and extend deep into eternity. Covenants are as personal as they are progressive. They bring light to darkness. They are healing and hopeful. They are heavenly evidence that God desperately wants to save all His children on both sides of the veil.

If you choose to read all the chapters, simply mark each example you can find of Jehovah and Abraham seeking a more personal relationship. Here are some examples of a covenant relationship from Abraham 2:

- Verse 3—The Lord warned Abraham and his family of danger.

- Verse 4—Sarah, Abraham, and others followed the Lord.

- Verse 6—The Lord appeared to Abraham and Lot in answer to their prayer.

- Verse 9—The Lord has significant purpose for those, like Abraham, who choose to make and keep covenants.

---

62 Jacob 3:1.
63 John 16:33.

- Verse 10—The Lord uses His covenant children to help do His work of gathering.
- Verse 11—All of God's children are entitled to receive all the blessings of the gospel.
- Verse 12—Abraham testified, "Thy servant has sought thee earnestly; now I have found thee."
- Verse 13—"I will do well to hearken unto thy voice."
- Verse 16—"Eternity was our covering and our rock and our salvation."
- Verse 17—Abraham "built an altar . . . and made an offering unto the Lord."
- Verse 18—Abraham "offered sacrifice . . . and called on the Lord devoutly."
- Verse 19—The Lord appeared to Abraham in answer to his prayers.
- Verse 20—Abraham built another altar higher up on a mountain and called upon the Lord again.

(or google "The Prince of Peace: Find Lasting Peace through Jesus Christ")

There are *at least* thirteen pieces of evidence in Abraham 2 of the depth of a covenant relationship with God. As you look at the list above, which of these experiences do you have a personal testimony of? I could circle a few at this point in my life, but the one that is most profound and personal to me is when Abraham testified in verse 12, "Thy servant has sought thee earnestly; now I have found thee." I know what that feels like.

We know Abraham was blessed in many ways but also went through excruciating trials. The simple question I would like to ask Abraham is, Is it worth it? Is the kind of relationship you have with Jesus Christ really worth all the suffering and pain you and your family experienced?

This is the point of the Old Testament where I ask myself if it is worth it? Based on my experiences and my testimony of verse 12, I believe my suffering in this life is absolutely worth the relationship I have with my Heavenly Parents and my Savior, Jesus Christ. As you watch the following video, ask yourself if you think a deeply personal relationship with Jesus Christ is worth it.

Gospel Library -> Videos and Images -> Holiday Videos -> Easter Videos -> The Prince of Peace

FEBRUARY 14–20
"IS ANY THING TOO HARD FOR THE LORD?"
GENESIS 18–23

God's Message to Me from This Section

SARAH, MARY, AND JESUS (15 MINUTES)

Birth stories are as emotional as they are complex. Take a few minutes to discuss the birth stories of the people in your study group. What emotions did each of you feel? Can you think of a tragic birth story? Can you think of a miraculous birth story? In what ways is physical birth symbolic of spiritual rebirth?[64]

Scriptures have several deeply instructive stories about pregnancy and birth. Paul uses pregnancy and birth as a metaphor for the signs of the times and the Second Coming of Jesus Christ.[65] Stories of birth and barrenness teach principles of love, devotion, grief, abandonment, betrayal, faith, trust, humility, and sacrifice. Many biblical birth stories are difficult because they are also paradoxical. For example, after years of infertility, Hannah prayed desperately for a son only to consecrate her son's miraculous life to the Lord.[66] Because birth is so dramatic emotionally, physically, and spiritually, these birth stories should be prioritized as some of the most significant and instructive in scripture.

Sarah and Abraham are promised to be a family "of many nations," yet Sarah is unable to have children for about seventy years. Why would the Lord give this faithful couple such hopeful promises but leave them unfulfilled for so long? The worry and heartache of unfulfilled family promises is something many of us can relate to. But after all these years, three holy men visit Sarah and Abraham to bring good tidings of great joy! Read Genesis 18:10–14, looking for the promise and Sarah's response to the news. (The word *laugh* used in Genesis 18:13 and 21:6 comes from the Hebrew word *tzachak*, which means both "to laugh" and "to rejoice"; thus, there is a double meaning implied in its use.[67]) Please mark the Lord's tender testimony: "Is there anything too hard for the Lord?"

Now let's use footnotes to make an incredible scripture connection. Footnote a in Genesis 18:14 refers us to a very similar but even more miraculous birth announcement, that of the angel Gabriel to Mary, soon to be the mortal mother of Jesus. After receiving the paradoxical news that Mary will bear a son even though she knew "not a man," Gabriel testified, "For with God nothing shall be impossible." This simple testimony must have been exactly what Mary needed because she immediately

---

64 For help, see John 3:3–5; Mosiah 5:5–10; Alma 7:14–16; Alma 19:6, 33; Moses 6:59–60.

65 1 Thessalonians 5:1–6.

66 1 Samuel 1:5–20.

67 See Genesis 21:6, footnote a.

accepts: "Behold, the handmaid of the Lord; be it unto me according to thy word."[68]

Now put these two heavenly testimonies together:
    "Is there anything too hard for the Lord?"
    "For with God nothing shall be impossible."

Both women have questions, both are confused by the seemingly impossible invitation and promise, and both are reassured by essentially the same heavenly testimony! Could it be that young Mary already knew Sarah's miraculous birth story? Did the angel quote a scripture Mary already had a burning testimony of? Was Genesis 18:14 a scripture Mary memorized in seminary? Did she attend a girls camp where the theme on all the T-shirts read, "Is there anything too hard for the Lord?" Was Mary's attention immediately turned to the miracle of Sarah, thus giving her the faith and trust to follow and accept a seemingly impossible invitation? It is impossible for me to definitively prove, but the consistency and connection of these verses cannot be overlooked.

Now that I'm already speculating, let me take my speculations one step further. Jesus was born into a home where Mary already had a deep testimony that "with God, nothing shall be impossible." If any human on the planet knew this by personal experience, it would be young Mary. Wouldn't it be probable to assume she taught Jesus and the rest of her children this truth? Jesus must have grown up in a "with God, nothing is impossible" home.

Interestingly, Jesus shared this same testimony during His mortal ministry. Recall the story of Jesus's interaction with the rich young ruler. After teaching this young man, "If thou wilt be perfect, go and sell that thou hast, and give to the poor, and thou shalt have treasure in heaven: and come and follow me," the young man "went away sorrowful: for he had great possessions." After the man left, Jesus reflected, "Verily I say unto you, That a rich man shall hardly enter into the kingdom of heaven. And again I say unto you, It is easier for a camel to go through the eye of a needle, than for a rich man to enter into the kingdom of God." The lingering disciples questioned, "Who then can be saved?" Jesus testified, "With men this is impossible; *but with God all things are possible*."[69]

Is Jesus echoing the testimony of his mortal mother? We rightly attribute God and angels for the divine development of the mortal Christ. I believe, at least in this instance, Mary taught Jesus that *all things are possible*.

Let me finish by adding one final, essential evidence of the eternal impact of Mary's teachings on the mortal Jesus. When faced with the agony of Gethsemane, Jesus was clearly shaken. The anguish, pain, and heaviness of His suffering was almost more than even His infinite shoulders could bear. As He searched for continuing motivation so as to not "shrink,"[70] I can picture the loving influence of Mary washing over His heart because it seems He quoted her again! At this critical point, Jesus cried out to the Father, "Remove this cup from me: nevertheless *not my will, but thine, be done*."[71] Roughly 34 years earlier, teenage Mary similarly submitted to the will of God, "Be it unto me according to thy word."[72] As Jesus bore the overwhelming pain of humanity, I believe He drew significant strength from the mortal mother who physically bore Him.

> Mary: "Be it unto me according to thy word."
>
> Jesus: "Nevertheless not my will, but thine, be done."

Similarly, are there any significant principles a parent, or parental figure, taught you that have helped you draw uncommon strength to overcome adversity?

SACRIFICE (10 MINUTES)

Using the chart below, list at least three scripture heroes or heroines. If you study with a group, have each person choose at least one. If you have small children, have them draw this person. After you have selected your hero/heroine, take two minutes to write all the ways they sacrificed for their faith in Jesus Christ.

Scripture Hero/ Heroine	Evidence of Sacrifice

---

68 Luke 1:34, 37–38.
69 Matthew 19:16–26, emphasis added.
70 Doctrine and Covenants 19:16–19.
71 Luke 22:42, emphasis added.
72 Luke 1:38.

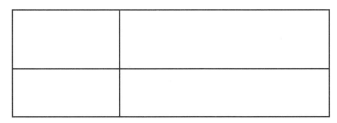

In Genesis 22:1–18, Abraham is commanded to sacrifice his promised son, Isaac. Interestingly, there are two words used for children in Hebrew. One signifies young children, and the other signifies teenagers and young adults. The word used for Isaac here informs us that he was a young adult. Since Abraham was well over 100 years old at this time, it is reasonable to assume Isaac could have easily escaped Abraham's capture if he chose to. Interestingly, Isaac submitted to the will of Abraham.[73]

Read the following quote and scriptures as you ponder these questions:

- In what ways is sacrifice an attribute of Heavenly Father and Jesus Christ?

- What connection do sacrifice and priorities share?

- What sacrifices have you made that have made a noticeable difference in your life?

- Are there ways we might oversacrifice, meaning how can we take this principle too far and sacrifice in ways that are beyond what God has asked?

President Nelson reframed the principle of sacrifice this way: "The question for each of us, regardless of race, is the same. Are *you* willing to let God prevail in your life? Are *you* willing to let God be the most important influence in your life? Will you allow His words, His commandments, and His covenants to influence what you do each day? Will you allow His voice to take priority over any other? Are you *willing* to let whatever He needs you to do take precedence over every other ambition? Are you *willing* to have your will swallowed up in His?"[74]

- Mark 12:41–44

- Doctrine and Covenants 97:8

- Doctrine and Covenants 64:33–34

- 1 Nephi 3:7

SACRIFICE, COVENANTS, LOVE (15 MINUTES)

Who is a person in scripture who reminds you the most of Jesus? What is it about them that reflects the Savior?

The lives of prophets often reflect and highlight certain aspects of the mission and purpose of Jesus Christ. Fill in the blank spaces in the following chart below. As you do, identify and analyze many of the similarities of the purpose and mission of Christ with the Abrahamic sacrifice of Isaac.[75]

Finding Jesus Christ Is the Test of Abraham		
	Symbolizes	Christ's birth was prophesied (Isaiah 7:14; Luke 1:31).
Isaac was born miraculously (Genesis 21:1–2).	Symbolizes	Christ was born miraculously (Luke 1:31; 1 Nephi 11:19–20).
Abraham was told to sacrifice one called his only begotten son (Genesis 22:12; Hebrew 11:17).	Symbolizes	
	Symbolizes	When Christ was called by God to sacrifice Himself, He answered, "Here am I" (Abraham 3:27).
Isaac carried the wood for the sacrifice on his back (JST Genesis 22:7).	Symbolizes	Christ carried the cross on His back (John 19:17).

---

73 See Kerry Muhlestein, *The Essential Old Testament Companion* (American Fork, UT: Covenant Communications, 2013), 48.
74 "Let God Prevail," *Liahona*, November 2020, 94.

75 Adapted from Kerry Muhlestein, *The Essential Old Testament Companion*, 49.

Abraham did not withhold his son from God (Genesis 22:12).	Symbolizes	God did not withhold His Son from us (Doctrine and Covenants 19:18–19).
As a result of his sacrifice, Abraham is promised innumerable seed (Genesis 22:17).	Symbolizes	
It was a three-day journey home from the place of sacrifice (Genesis 22:4).	Symbolizes	Christ was in the spirit world for three days after His sacrifice (Mosiah 3:10).

Options to fill in the table:

- When God called Abraham to make the sacrifice, Abraham answered, "Here I am" (Genesis 22:1).

- As a result of His sacrifice, Christ will have innumerable seed (Mosiah 15:10–12).

- Isaac's birth was prophesied (Genesis 17:16).

- God sacrifices His Only Begotten Son (John 3:16).

Similarly, Moses was told in vision that he was "in similitude of mine Only Begotten." In fact, Moses used this same testimony twice to combat the personal attack Satan waged upon him.[76] There are many ways Moses is similar to Jesus Christ, especially as a gatherer, liberator, and lawgiver. Like Abraham and Moses, isn't anyone who intentionally attempts to keep their covenants through sacrifice in similitude of the Only Begotten?[77]

Read the baptismal covenant that Alma explained at the waters of Mormon. Mark all aspects of this covenant that invite us to choose to sacrifice:

> And it came to pass that he said unto them: Behold, here are the waters of Mormon (for thus were they called) and now, as ye are desirous to come into the fold of God, and to be called his people,

and are willing to bear one another's burdens, that they may be light;

Yea, and are willing to mourn with those that mourn; yea, and comfort those that stand in need of comfort, and to stand as witnesses of God at all times and in all things, and in all places that ye may be in, even until death, that ye may be redeemed of God, and be numbered with those of the first resurrection, that ye may have eternal life—

Now I say unto you, if this be the desire of your hearts, what have you against being baptized in the name of the Lord, as a witness before him that ye have entered into a covenant with him, that ye will serve him and keep his commandments, that he may pour out his Spirit more abundantly upon you?[78]

Let me ask the same question in two different ways:

- In what ways are *you* like Jesus Christ?

- In what ways are *you* intentionally trying to keep your covenants?

Jesus Christ is a covenant keeper! How do you see sacrifice, covenant keeping, and the Savior's love in the following video about an Abrahamic trial?

Gospel Library -> Video and Images -> Inspirational Messages -> Feeling the Lord's Love and Goodness in Trials

(or google "Feeling the Lord's Love and Goodness in Trials")

---

76 Moses 1:6, 13, 16.
77 Mosiah 5:5–15.

78 Mosiah 18:8–10.

FEBRUARY 21–27
THE COVENANT IS RENEWED
GENESIS 24–27

_____

God's Message to Me from This Section

_____

CAMELS AND NAVY SEALS (10 MINUTES)

If you have small children, you may want to have them build a camel out of Legos or blocks, or you could have them draw a picture of a camel. Here are some interesting facts about camels:

- Camels can easily carry 200 pounds of extra weight and walk about 20 miles per day through a harsh desert climate.

- Camels can grow up to 6.6 feet at the shoulders and weigh over 1,300 pounds.

- Camels have a double row of extra-long eyelashes to help keep sand out of their eyes, and they can close their nostrils to keep sand out.

- Camels can go without water for several weeks. They only sweat at 106 degrees Fahrenheit.

- Camels live for an average of 18 years.[79]

As Isaac aged to maturity, it became important for him to marry. Abraham sent out his chief servant to find a woman Isaac could marry from Abraham's family to ensure the covenant continued through future generations. Abraham's chief servant traveled a long distance to Mesopotamia. Obviously nervous about the magnitude of the task, the servant asked God to help him.

This servant was searching for a specific sign that one of the women at the well where he stopped would show charity to him by fetching water for himself as well as his camels. Culturally, it was expected that if someone asked for a drink at the well, it would be unthinkable not to help. But if the person offered to assist with the camels, it showed the person's willingness to serve and offer charity to a stranger.

"Before he had done speaking . . . Rebekah came out" (Genesis 24:15).

Rebekah gave Abraham's servant water and then freely offered to help draw water for the camels (see Genesis 24:17–21). Let's analyze Rebekah's natural willingness to help others. Have you ever wondered how much water she had to draw to quench the thirst of Abraham's servant *and* his ten camels? Here's some additional camel facts that prove Rebekah's heavenly character as a *Divine Helper*:[80]

- On a long-distance trip, camels drink about thirty gallons of water to rehydrate.

- Thirty gallons of water multiplied by ten camels is 300 gallons of water.

_____

79 PBS Nature Blog, "Camel Fact Sheet," September 17, 2020.

80 See January 3–9 lesson to note the similarities of Eve and Jesus as *helpers*.

- One gallon of water weighs approximately 8.3 pounds.
- Rebekah reasonably would have volunteered to fetch, or at least assisted in fetching, 2,490 pounds of extra water than what was culturally required!

I think we should change the commonly quoted "go the extra mile" to "carry the extra 2,490 pounds of water." But in all seriousness, think about how Rebekah's natural charity spoke volumes of her Christ-like character.

Now, if you have anxiety and depression like I do, this story will overwhelm you! "How can I carry so much weight in the service of others when I can barely get out of bed today?" For me, I don't usually think of it as carrying 2,490 pounds of service at once. I think of carrying only two or three pounds one time. Then I do it again and again and again. Some days, I can carry twenty pounds, other days I can only carry a few ounces. Over the course of one month, I can look back and see that with God's help, I accomplished a lot more than I ever thought possible.

The Church of Jesus Christ of Latter-day Saints is designed based on this mentality. For example, taking the sacrament this week may not change your life, but if you are mostly active in the Church for twenty-five years, you will have taken the sacrament over 1,100 times. That can make a difference! Especially when you consider 200 members of your congregation doing the same thing over twenty-five years. The small crust of bread and the few drops of water over time represent significant spiritual power in our personal lives and in our communities.

Daily scripture study, prayer, *Come, Follow Me*, ministering, and callings are all patterned after disciples like Rebekah. Alma the Younger was a Rebekah-like disciple of Christ when he taught his son Helaman (I'm paraphrasing only a little), "You may think what I am about to say is dumb, but I say unto you, that by small and simple things are great things brought to pass."[81]

Take a few minutes to reflect on the small and simple things you have done so far this year. What actions have served you? What actions have not? Is there one small, simple thing you can do this week that over time could make a real difference?

For inspiration, please watch this Navy SEAL testify of this same principle:

(or google "Navy Seal Admiral Shares Reasons to Make Bed Everyday")

WHAT DO I DO WHEN . . . ? (20 MINUTES)

The story of Esau selling something as important as his birthright for something as trivial as a bowl of soup is used as a common life lesson. The moral of the story: placing worldly, or immediate, desires above eternal priorities will eventually lead to sorrow and regret (see Genesis 25:29–32). As with many stories in the Bible, we should be careful to not take this one incident and assume it happened only one time, in isolation. Usually, the writer includes one story as an example of a pattern of behavior or to highlight certain useful or not useful characteristics. In the last section, the author included one story of Rebekah's remarkable character. Clearly, this was not the only time she treated someone in a Christ-like way. It was one example that represented her mostly charitable personality. Similarly, though Esau sold his birthright in this one example, be careful *not* to assume that he messed up *one time* and was cut off from the Lord's divine influence and blessings *forever*. It is one example used to teach us in brevity that over time, Esau did not value God's precious promises.

Additionally, Jacob and Esau are twins. Rather than thinking of them as two totally separate people, think of them as one person with both Jacob desires and Esau desires "struggling together within" (Genesis 25:22). This is the same thing I mentioned earlier in the book when you look at Cain and Abel, and Laman and Nephi.[82] The real questions are more about what I value. Jacob values a life dedicated to service and obedience to God and his fellow man—a covenant path. Esau represents a life dedicated to others serving and being obedient to him—a "me first" path.

All of us to some extent figuratively sell our birthright for a mess of pottage. When this happens, our next belief is often that we simply can't come back. This belief

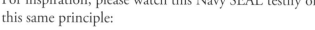

81 Alma 37:6.

82 See January 10–16 lesson.

leads to shame. We believe we are unsavable, unlovable, unchangeable, and destined for darkness and sadness because that's what we deserve. From my own experience, I have learned that certain forms of mental illness can amplify these feelings until they are almost unbearable. The parable of the Prodigal Son is a fantastic illustration that this "*point of no return*" belief is powerful—but it also illustrates that it is *not* true.[83]

Instead of using Esau as a reason to beat ourselves up because we've messed up, my hope is to show how we can change to become more like Jacob. Let's talk about what we do *when* we find ourselves becoming more like Esau. What do we do *when* we keep falling short and feel like there is no hope for us? What do we do *when*, not *if*, we are struggling to stay on the path? Let me share three truths that can help. Please write down any others that may come to mind for you.

TRUTH #1—IT IS NOT TIME TO GIVE UP; IT IS TIME TO STEP UP :)

Esau "despised his birthright" (Genesis 25:34), but rather than course-correcting, he continued to fight against change. He blamed Jacob for his own personal choices. Hearing God's voice became less and less valuable to Esau.

- "Jacob . . . hath supplanted me these two times: he took away my birthright; and, behold, now he hath taken away my blessings" (Genesis 27:36).

- "Esau hated Jacob because of the blessing where-with his father blessed him" (Genesis 27:41).

- Esau thought killing Jacob would bring him comfort (see Genesis 27:42). He tried to find comfort in revenge, not repentance.

- Esau chose instead to make relationships with those who also despised a relationship with God (see Genesis 26:34).

TRUTH #2—GOD IS WITH YOU EVEN IF YOUR CHOICES HAVE MADE IT HARD FOR YOU TO FEEL HIS LOVING INFLUENCE.

To understand this truth, watch the following video and notice that God was with Mark even when Mark made poor decisions.

Gospel Library -> Videos and Images -> Inspirational Videos -> The Savior Wants to Forgive

(or google "The Savior Wants to Forgive")

TRUTH #3—YOU ARE SAVED BECAUSE JESUS IS PERFECT, NOT BECAUSE YOU ARE.

This truth is not meant to make you feel bad but to allow you to release the burden of unrealistic expectations. If perfection were required of us, we wouldn't need Jesus because we would simply save ourselves. Life experience clearly teaches us that perfection is not possible anyway. We are saved through the grace of Jesus, fully and completely.

Jacob, Nephi's righteous little brother, learned he could not save himself, and he was nothing like Esau; he was awesome! As you read the following verse, notice *whose* righteousness redeemed Jacob: "Wherefore, thy soul shall be blessed, and thou shalt dwell safely with thy brother, Nephi; and thy days shall be spent in the service of thy God. Wherefore, I know that thou art redeemed, *because of the righteousness of thy Redeemer*."[84]

So a better question is not whether you can become perfect but whether or not you will consistently choose to try to have a relationship with Jesus Christ in spite of your imperfections.

---

83 Luke 15:11–32.

84 2 Nephi 2:3, emphasis added.

FEBRUARY 28–MARCH 6
"SURELY THE LORD IS IN THIS PLACE"
GENESIS 28–33

God's Message to Me from This Section

BIRTH*RIGHT*? MORE LIKE BIRTH*FIGHT* (5 MINUTES)

Understanding the basics of what the birthright meant to families in Old Testament culture is important. The birthright was most often passed from father to oldest son, but exceptions could be made. The basic core of the birthright blessing was based on two primary responsibilities:

1. *Leadership*—The birthright child inherited leadership responsibilities to take care of the family, especially those who could not take care of themselves. This would include aging parents, widows, orphans, and even extended family.

2. *Land*—The birthright child would get a double inheritance to give them the resources to fulfill their additional family responsibilities.

The birthright being transferred to the oldest son was symbolic of Jesus Christ being the *Firstborn* child of God, chosen to lead God's family to eternal safety and peace. "Because I Have Been Given Much" is a great hymn that describes the purpose and responsibility of the birthright child.

For members of The Church of Jesus Christ of Latter-day Saints, the cultural impact of who receives the birthright is easier to recognize in the Book of Mormon.

Interestingly, seventy-six percent of the pages of the Book of Mormon are written before the birth of Jesus Christ, so we can better understand many Old Testament themes by including Book of Mormon knowledge. The importance of the birthright in Old Testament culture is displayed from the beginning pages. In Sariah and Lehi's family, the obvious birthright child was Laman. It is clear Laman was intelligent, driven, assertive, and influential. Additionally, Sariah and Lehi were clearly wealthy, and Laman knew from early childhood that he would one day take majority ownership of the family's wealth. Laman had won the lottery!

When Lehi was commanded to leave his land and position of leadership in Jerusalem and take up a tent in the desert, Laman was not just giving up some general conveniences. He was giving up the wealth and influence of being Lehi's birthright son! This is most likely the reason he and Lemuel murmur so much.

What complicates matters further is a very important interaction Nephi had with the Lord just before the family left Jerusalem. As Nephi was praying to understand why they needed to leave, the Lord visited him and softened his heart to believe Lehi. As we read further, it looks like the Lord transferred the birthright to Nephi. Remember, birthright is primarily *land* and *leadership*. The Lord gave Nephi a *land* inheritance: "And inasmuch as ye shall keep my commandments, ye shall prosper, and shall be led to a *land of promise*; yea, even a *land* which I have prepared for you; yea, a *land* which is choice above all other *lands*." And two verses later, Nephi received a *leadership* inheritance: "And inasmuch as thou shalt keep my commandments, thou shalt be made *a ruler and a teacher over thy brethren*."[85]

Fast-forward to when Nephi convinced his brothers to use their left-behind wealth—or as Laman saw it, *his* wealth—to buy the plates of brass from Laban. They lost their wealth and almost lost their lives. After they fled to safety in the cavity of a rock, Laman had a violent, abusive reaction, but why? Laman finally fully realized that his birthright inheritance was gone, and it was all Nephi's fault! When the angel of the Lord appeared and stopped the abuse, he clearly taught Laman, "Why do ye smite your younger brother with a rod? Know ye not that the Lord hath chosen him to be a *ruler* over you, and this because of your iniquities?"[86] In other words, the angel just confirmed to Laman that he had indeed lost his birthright to Nephi, and it was his own fault. Who is entitled to the birthright, Laman or Nephi, is at the core of the Nephite/Lamanite wars and battles.[87]

Wars fought in the Old Testament are often over birthright issues as well. As Esau broke away from Jacob, his descendants became known as Edomites, who would fight against Jacob's descendants from time to time, just like the Lamanites would do to the Nephites.[88]

GAME TIME! (20 MINUTES)

First—If you study as a family or group, take a few minutes to play Pictionary. (If you are studying alone, get out a piece of paper and draw your interpretation of Genesis 28:12–19.) Pictionary is played by splitting your group into two teams. Each team picks someone to draw a picture. The rest of the team does not know what the picture is. The person has thirty seconds to draw the picture and get their team to guess it correctly. If they

are successful, their team gets a point. Please adapt this if you have small children. My young kids love playing scripture Pictionary!

Pictionary words:

- Earth
- Heaven
- Gift
- Ladder
- Angels
- Temple
- Pillow

Genesis 28:12–19 is very significant because as Jacob was both fleeing for his life and searching for a wife, he had a dream. As you read these verses, mark all the words from playing Pictionary that show up in Jacob's dream.

Second—Have someone draw the dream of Jacob's ladder. What do you think Jacob might have learned from the image of a ladder extending from earth to the Lord's presence? For example, while climbing a ladder, we move farther away from some things as we move closer to other things.

President Marion G. Romney of the Quorum of the Twelve Apostles taught, "Jacob realized that the covenants he made with the Lord there were the rungs on the ladder that he himself would have to climb in order to obtain the promised blessings—blessings that would entitle him to enter heaven and associate with the Lord."[89]

Although there are many priesthood ordinances performed in the Church today, only a few are considered *saving* ordinances. All other ordinances have their purpose and importance but are not essential for salvation. Saving ordinances are essential for salvation with our Heavenly Parents. They are:

- Baptism by immersion
- Confirmation and receiving the Holy Ghost
- Conferring the priesthood and ordaining to priesthood office (for men only)
- Initiatory and endowment in the temple
- Marriage sealing in the temple

---

85 1 Nephi 2:16–22, *emphasis added*.

86 1 Nephi 3:16–31, *emphasis added*.

87 For additional evidence, read Mosiah 10:11–18. These verses are a summary of why the Lamanites hate the Nephites so much, even 400 years later. In Mosiah 10:16, it states that the Lamanites felt that they had been robbed. Robbed of what? The birthright blessing of land and leadership.

88 See Genesis 25:22–23; 1 Nephi 2:23–24.

89 "Temples—The Gates to Heaven," *Ensign*, March 1971, 16.

Now mark verse 14 and link it to Abraham 2:9–11. The Lord is renewing the Abrahamic Covenant and promises with Jacob. Interestingly, the Lord does all of this *before*, not *after*, Jacob is married.

Third—Read through Genesis 28:12–19 again and mark all the phrases that attach covenant keeping with a relationship with Jesus Christ. Here is what I found:

- The Lord speaks to Jacob.
- Angels are all along the covenant path, both ascending and descending.
- The Lord has gifts and blessings to give families.
- "I am with thee."
- "[I] will keep thee in all places."
- "[I] will bring [restore] thee again."
- "I will not leave thee."

Fourth—Because of this sacred experience, Jacob used a stone and oil to dedicate the land where he had this incredible dream. He also gave the land a new name: Beth-el.

President Marion G. Romney continued: "Because he had met the Lord and entered into covenants with him there, Jacob considered the site so sacred that he named the place Bethel, a contraction of Beth-Elohim, which means literally "the House of the Lord." He said of it: "This is none other but the house of God, and this is the gate of heaven. . . . Temples are to us all what Bethel was to Jacob. Even more, they are also the gates to heaven for all of our unendowed kindred dead. We should all do our duty in bringing our loved ones through them."[90]

CHILDREN OF ISRAEL (5 MINUTES)

Jacob ended up marrying both daughters of Laban (no, not the Laban from the Book of Mormon). Their names are Leah and Rachel. Leah and Rachel both had handmaids, Zilpah and Bilhah, who were also married to Jacob. Leah and Rachel would be considered wives to Jacob, Zilpah and Bilhah were considered concubines. In Old Testament culture, a concubine was legally married to a man but was distinguished as belonging to a lower class.

After Jacob wrestled with a messenger of God, God changed his name to Israel. *Israel* in Hebrew means "let God prevail" (see Genesis 32:24–28).

Here is a way to help you see the children of Israel organized by birth mothers. The number to the left identifies the order of children born from 1–13 (oldest to youngest).[91]

Leah (older sister)	Zilpah (Leah's handmaid)	Bilhah (Rachel's handmaid)	Rachel (younger sister)
1– Reuben	7– Gad	5– Dan	12– Joseph
2– Simeon	8– Asher	6– Naphtali	13–Benjamin
3– Levi			
4– Judah			
9– Issachar			
10– Zebulun			
11–Dinah (only daughter of Israel)			

The house, or family, of Israel is the most prominent family in the Old Testament. They made such an impact on the earth that we are still talking about them today! This family must have been perfect, right? Well, perfection isn't possible so at the very least, they must be the *ideal* family that we should all emulate. As you finish the book of Genesis, you will notice this is far from true. Unless I am mistaken, God did not waste a single page of scripture showing us the perfect family. Like all families, the family of Israel is filled with good and bad, complicated and simple, faithful and faithless, and everything in between. The family of Israel essentially represents *every* family. Every time I finish the book of Genesis, I think, "If God didn't give up on *that* family, surely he won't give up on mine!" As you read Genesis 30–33, look for evidence of the injustice, confusion, and heartache members of this family endured. Also notice the hand of the Lord in their lives.

---

90 *ibid.*

91 See Genesis 29:32–35; 30:5–13, 17–25.

MARCH 7–13

"THE LORD WAS WITH JOSEPH"

GENESIS 37–41

MARCH 14–20

"GOD MEANT IT UNTO GOOD"

GENESIS 42–50

God's Message to Me from This Section

You read the heading correctly. I am combining the next two weeks of content into one section in this book.

TBH (TO BE HONEST) (20 MINUTES)

Be honest:

Would you rather *read* the scriptures or *watch* the scriptures?

One of my favorite attributes of God is that He is "a God of truth, and canst not lie."[92] In trying to be more like God, I want to be as truthful as I can. In my honesty, I must confess that this week of Come, Follow Me will mostly include watching DreamWorks's *Joseph: King of Dreams* (2000). It is one of my favorite DreamWorks movies of all time. We will get each person's favorite movie snack and drink and enjoy this movie together. We may even watch it twice—the first time for fun and the second time to really ask questions, discuss highlights, and learn.

My favorite way to understand Joseph is to view him as a type for Jesus Christ. Please use the following chart to ensure you see the Savior in Joseph's life.[93]

Joseph Sold into Egypt as a Type of Jesus Christ	
Joseph	**Jesus**
Was loved by his father (Genesis 37:3).	Was loved by His Father (Doctrine and Covenants 76:25).
Obedient to his father, responding, "Here am I" (Genesis 37:13)	Fully obedient to His Father, responding, "Here am I" (Abraham 3:27).
Promised to be a great ruler (Genesis 37:5–11).	Promised to be a great ruler (Isaiah 9:6).
Betrayed by his brothers and stripped of his garments (Genesis 37:23–28).	Betrayed and was stripped of his garments (Mark 14:43–15:24).
Sold by Judah for twenty pieces of silver, the price of a child slave (Genesis 37:26–28).	Sold by Judas (Greek for *Judah*) for thirty pieces of silver, the price of an adult slave (Matthew 26:15).

---

92 Ether 3:12; see also Enos 1:6.
93 Adapted from Kerry Muhlestein, *The Essential Old Testament Companion*, 85.

Was consistently tempted but refused (Genesis 39:7–12).	Was consistently tempted but refused (Matthew 4:1–11).
Was falsely accused by Potiphar's wife (Genesis 39:17–18).	Was falsely accused before the Sanhedrin (Matthew 26:59).
Was thirty years old when he began his life's work (Genesis 41:46).	Was thirty years old when He began His ministry (Luke 3:23).
Chose to forgive those who caused him pain (Genesis 50:20–21).	Chose to forgive those who caused Him pain (Luke 23:34).
Saved his family from certain death (Genesis 45).	Saved the family of God from death and hell (2 Nephi 9:19–21).
Gathered the scattered family of Israel (Genesis 45).	Will gather the scattered house of Israel (Isaiah 54:7).
Served in prison, then elevated to Pharaoh's second in command (Genesis 40–41).	Taught in spirit prison, then was elevated to God's right hand (1 Peter 3:19; Acts 5:31).
People from many nations bowed before him (Genesis 41:43).	All people and nations will bow before Him (Philippians 2:10).
Suffered greatly when separated from his father (Genesis 45:3).	Suffered greatly when separated from His Father (Matthew 27:46).
After trials, was reunited with his father (Genesis 46:29–30).	After trials, was reunited with His Father (Mark 16:19).
Gave his family an inheritance (Genesis 47:11).	Gives us an eternal inheritance (John 14:2–3).

JOSEPH'S LIFE—A PATTERN OF THE PLAN OF SALVATION (15 MINUTES)

The basic pattern of Joseph's life follows the pattern of the plan of salvation. Obviously, some elements don't fit perfectly. For example, Joseph was forced to leave his home against his will. We were not forced to leave our heavenly home against our will. Recognizing patterns like this is also useful to make sense of the temple endowment because it follows the pattern of the plan of salvation as well using Adam and Eve as our representatives instead of Joseph.

PREMORTAL LIFE

Joseph lived with his entire family in the physical presence of his father and mother just as we did in premortality. He was instructed and tried to be obedient.

MORTAL LIFE

Joseph left the presence of his parents and experienced extreme difficulty and loneliness as he longed to be back with his parents. He was imprisoned, delivered, betrayed, and given spiritual gifts to help him eventually overcome the difficulties he would face. He found both joy and heartache in his relationships with others. Joseph's life in Egypt represents a fallen mortal experience.

POSTMORTAL SPIRIT WORLD

In keeping his covenants and rising above the challenges he faced by relying on and recognizing God's help in his life, Joseph was prepared to help gather his family and deliver them from famine. Covenant keepers on both sides of the veil help to gather Israel and save them through the Atonement of Jesus Christ.

MILLENNIUM AND HEAVEN

Notice the similarities of John the Beloved's description of the millennium, Enoch's Zion returning to earth, and Joseph and his brother's family reunion:

John the Beloved	The Return of Enoch's Zion	Joseph's Family Reunion
Revelation 21:2–4	Moses 7:62–63	Genesis 45:4–5, 14–15
2 And I John saw the holy city, new Jerusalem, coming down from God out of heaven, prepared as a bride adorned for her husband.	62 For there shall be my tabernacle, and it shall be called Zion, a New Jerusalem.	4 And he said, I am Joseph your brother, whom ye sold into Egypt.
3 And I heard a great voice out of heaven saying, Behold, the tabernacle of God is with men, and he will dwell with them, and they shall be his people, and God himself shall be with them, and be their God.	63 And the Lord said unto Enoch: Then shalt thou and all thy city meet them there, and we will receive them into our bosom, and they shall see us; and we will fall upon their necks, and they shall fall upon our necks, and we will kiss each other.	5 Now therefore be not grieved, nor angry with yourselves, that ye sold me hither: for God did send me before you to preserve life.

14 And he fell upon his brother Benjamin's neck, and wept; and Benjamin wept upon his neck. |
| 4 And God shall wipe away all tears from their eyes; and there shall be no more death, neither sorrow, nor crying, neither shall there be any more pain: for the former things are passed away. | | 15 Moreover he kissed all his brethren, and wept upon them: and after that his brethren talked with him. |

THE UNIFYING POWER OF FORGIVENESS (10 MINUTES)

One of the powerful messages in the story of Joseph sold into Egypt is forgiveness. In Doctrine and Covenants 64:9–10, the Lord defines three types of forgiveness: forgiveness from God, forgiveness of others, and forgiveness of self. It might be important to find time during these two weeks to incorporate forgiveness into your home. One simple way to do this is to incorporate a daily habit of praying for and seeking forgiveness in these three ways. This video is a fun resource to use to promote a positive discussion about forgiveness.

(Gospel Library -> Videos and Images -> Inspirational Messages -> The Goal: A Story of Faith, Friendship, and Forgiveness)

(or google "The Goal: A Story of Faith, Friendship and Forgiveness")

MARCH 21–27
"I HAVE REMEMBERED MY COVENANT"
EXODUS 1–6

God's Message to Me from This Section

EXODUS OVERVIEW

Exodus begins about 400 years after Genesis ends. Read Exodus 1:6–14 to understand why the Israelites went from their esteemed position when Joseph ruled in Egypt to a massive group of enslaved labor in desperate need of a liberator. This liberator will be Moses. The word *Exodus* in Greek means "a departure." Exodus is divided into two major sections:

1. Chapters 1–18 describe the historical liberation of the Israelites from Egypt.

2. Chapters 19–40 describe the Lord's invitation of spiritual liberation from sin and death.

The book of Exodus spans from the death of Joseph until just after the Exodus (about 1671 BC to 1547 BC). We know Moses has the keys of the gathering of Israel because he conferred them on Joseph Smith in the Kirtland Temple in April 1836.[94] It is probable that Moses received these priesthood keys when he received his calling from the Lord during the burning-bush experience.[95]

"ENCIRCLED IN THE ARMS OF SAFETY" (10 MINUTES)

In three minutes or less, go around your home and identify all the things you can that are meant to protect you and keep you safe. If you have kids with cell phones, have them take a picture of each item they find. After three minutes, come back together to discuss what you found. What does each of these items protect you from? How effective are they?

The Hebrew word used most often to describe the Atonement of Jesus Christ is *kafar*, which basically means "to cover, to pass over, to forgive."[96] In the New Testament, the word *save* is most often translated from the Greek word *sozo*. *Sozo* means "to heal, save, preserve, or rescue from destruction by bringing into divine safety."[97]

In Exodus 2:1–10, we get the story of how Moses was miraculously saved by his mother when she made "an ark," or a small box, to save him from the death decree of Pharaoh. Just like Noah's ark, and similar to the Jaredite barges, this ark was meant to *kafar* Moses from the Pharaoh and *sozo* him in the river! In a previous lesson, we discussed the symbolism of Noah's ark and our modern temples.[98] I now want to take Moses's little ark and liken it to being covered by the safety and protection of our personal covenants, symbolized by the garments of the holy priesthood.

---

94 See Doctrine and Covenants 110:11.
95 See Exodus 3:1–15.
96 Hugh Nibley, "The Atonement of Jesus Christ, Part 1," *Ensign*, July 1990.
97 *Bible Hub*, s.v. "sozo," https://biblehub.com/greek/4982.htm.
98 See January 31–February 6 lesson.

Notice a similar tone in Amulek's powerful and metaphorical teachings of the Atonement: "And thus mercy can satisfy the demands of justice, and encircles them in the arms of *safety*, while he that exercises no faith unto repentance is *exposed* to the whole law of the demands of justice; therefore only unto him that has faith unto repentance is brought about the great and eternal plan of redemption."[99]

Although keeping covenants is no guarantee that life will be easy, it is a guarantee that there is always hope through the Savior, Jesus Christ.

Can you think of an experience where you felt protected by Christ?

After watching the following video, write one sentence that describes what you learned today that you hope to remember.

Gospel Library -> Videos and Images -> Inspirational Videos -> Spiritual Whirlwinds

(or google "Spiritual Whirlwinds")

PLAY THE "FAVORITES GAME"! (15 MINUTES)

What is your favorite in each of the following categories? Move through these questions quickly. If you study with a group, have everyone answer the first question, then move on to the second and have everyone answer that one, and so on.

- Favorite home-cooked meal?
- Favorite article of clothing?
- Favorite book?
- Favorite app on your phone?
- Favorite thing to draw?
- Favorite place you've lived?

- Favorite song?
- Favorite beverage?

As the Lord called and tutored Moses, He identified many attributes Moses possessed that motivated him to help the enslaved children of Israel. Coming to know the character of the God who supports us in our lives can be very motivating. Fill in these attributes in the blanks below and mark them in your scriptures.

Exodus 2:24	God hears our groanings; God remembers us
Exodus 2:25	God sees us; God knows and is aware of us (see footnote 25a)
Exodus 3:4	
Exodus 3:5	
Exodus 3:7	
Exodus 3:8	God will *come down* to deliver us so He can *bring us up*
Exodus 3:9	
Exodus 3:10	God will use us to help others even if it seems impossible
Exodus 3:11	
Exodus 3:16	
Exodus 3:17	
Exodus 3:20	
Exodus 3:21	Even when we fail, we are never empty or alone

If you had to pick one, which one of these attributes of God is your favorite? If you feel it could be effective, have the people in your group draw a picture that can help them remember this attribute of God for the week.

99 Alma 34:16, emphasis added.

MARCH 28–APRIL 3
"REMEMBER THIS DAY, IN WHICH YE CAME OUT FROM EGYPT"
EXODUS 7–13

God's Message to Me from This Section

FAITH & FAILURE (20 MINUTES)

Take a few minutes to brainstorm some of your recent failures. What are some of the things you've really worked at but you ultimately failed at?

I vividly remember interviewing for a job at a local bank when I was in my early twenties. During the interview with the bank manager, we discussed strengths and weaknesses. He asked me how I felt about failure. My response was, "I'd rather not try than try and fail." That is generally true of me then and now.

Most of my life I have had an adversarial relationship with failure. When I fail at something, especially if I've really tried, my initial response is to recoil with feelings of insecurity, self-doubt, embarrassment, and worthlessness. I want to hide. I want to disappear. When difficult failures compound one upon another, I feel like Peter, who once walked confidently on the water but then sank into the darkness of hopelessness and doubt.

When you experience failure, how do you feel? How have these feelings changed over the years?

Elder Lynn G. Robbins of the Presidency of the Seventy gave a talk in general conference where he specifically addressed failure and its role in the plan of salvation. Using the stories of Moses and Nephi, his words have significantly changed my relationship with failure for the better. He taught, "'Success,' it has been said, 'isn't the absence of failure, but going from failure to failure without any loss of enthusiasm.' With his invention of the light bulb, Thomas Edison purportedly said, 'I didn't fail 1,000 times. The light bulb was an invention with 1,000 steps.' . . . Hopefully, each mistake we make becomes a lesson in wisdom, turning stumbling blocks into stepping-stones. Nephi's unwavering faith helped him go from failure to failure until he finally obtained the brass plates. It took Moses *10 attempts* before he finally found success in fleeing Egypt with the Israelites."

Elder Robbins then asked questions that I have essentially asked for years: "We may wonder—if both Nephi and Moses were on the Lord's errand, why didn't the Lord intervene and help them achieve success on their first try? Why did He allow them—and why does He allow us—to flounder and fail in our attempts to succeed?"[100]

Have you ever asked questions like these as you have experienced failure and unmet expectations? Take a few minutes to see if you can come up with at least three faith-focused answers to these questions.

---

100 "Until Seventy Times Seventy," *Ensign*, May 2018, 21.

1. _____

   _____

2. _____

   _____

3. _____

   _____

After you have pondered Elder Robbins's questions, please watch the following parable of the piano given to us by BYU Religion Professor Brad Wilcox. This parable also helps redefine failure when it comes to our relationship with the expectations and grace of Jesus Christ.[101]

(Or google "Inspiring Short: His Grace Is Sufficient Brad Wilcox")

In conclusion, here are the four answers Elder Robbins gave to his questions:

- First, the Lord knows that "these things shall give [us] experience, and shall be for [our] good."

- Second, to allow us to "taste the bitter, that [we] may know to prize the good."

- Third, to prove that "the battle is the Lord's," and it is only by His grace that we can accomplish His work and become like Him.

- Fourth, to help us develop and hone scores of Christlike attributes that cannot be refined except through opposition and "in the furnace of affliction."

In summary, what is at least one thing you learned today that can help you have a healthier relationship with failure?

CAVES & COVENANTS (10 MINUTES)

Have you ever been in a cave? If not, what is the darkest place you've ever been? What was it like? How long were you in there before legitimate fear set in? What helped you feel safe?

One of the final plagues sent to Egypt was darkness, but this was no ordinary darkness: "And the Lord said unto Moses, Stretch out thine hand toward heaven, that there may be darkness over the land of Egypt, even darkness which may be felt. And Moses stretched forth his hand toward heaven; and there was a thick darkness in all the land of Egypt three days: They saw not one another, neither rose any from his place for three days."[102]

Symbolically, when there is thick darkness, there is no vision and no progression.

The next phrase in these scriptures is profound! I discovered it as a missionary over twenty years ago, and it has brought me comfort and hope ever since. It has helped me through so many dark experiences of my life. Why should I make and keep covenants? There are so many things that bother me in Church history and in current and past Church policies. Why should I stay? There is too much darkness in the world for God to exist; why should I believe?

While all felt the immobilizing darkness, the final phrase in Exodus 10:23 reads:

"But all the children of Israel had light in their dwellings."

I wonder if President Nelson would rewrite this to say, "But all those who let God prevail had light in their dwellings." Can you feel the truth, depth, hope, and importance of this promise?

Ten days before I left on my mission, four of my friends were in a serious car accident on their way to a concert. Unfortunately, one of them tragically passed away. Because my life changed so much right after his passing, the grief of his death did not fully impact me until after I was in the MTC for a few days. One night as I was lying in bed, the weight of his death and the reality of death overwhelmed me! I remember feeling deep sadness, grief, loss, and betrayal. Why would God allow the tragedies and sadness that surround death?

Coincidentally, I was in the process of rereading the Book of Mormon. In these feelings, I was prompted

---

101 From BYU Speeches, "His Grace Is Sufficient," July 12, 2011.

102 Exodus 10:21–22.

to read. My bookmark was in Mosiah 16. Soon after beginning, I read this testimony of Abinadi: "But there is a resurrection, therefore the grave hath no victory, and the sting of death is swallowed up in Christ." The profound sadness I was feeling was completely swept away as I read these verses. In my mind, I saw Christ with a loving smile, tear-soaked eyes, and His arms open, inviting me into a heavenly hug. It felt like Jesus was telling me, "It's okay! I love you. I overcame death for all." But it didn't stop there. This feeling of love and reassurance was amplified by the next verse. Instead of Abinadi's testimony of Christ, it was almost as if Jesus was testifying of Himself, "[I am] the light and the life of the world; yea, a light that is endless, that can never be darkened; yea, and also a life which is endless, that there can be no more death."[103] These verses have provided me with air when life experiences have felt suffocating, these verses have provided me with light in darkness, and these verses have provided me with hope when I have felt completely lost. I testify that Christ is the light that has, can, and will overcome any darkness we experience in mortality.

Please think about an experience where you were surrounded by thick darkness but you found Christ's light anyway. As you ponder, watch the following video and look for the light this young man found in the darkness he felt.

(Or google "Somebody to Stand by You Jeffrey R. Holland")

---

[103] Mosiah 16:8–9.

APRIL 4–10
"STAND STILL, AND SEE THE SALVATION OF THE LORD"
EXODUS 14–17

God's Message to Me from This Section

WILL THE LORD FIGHT FOR ME? (10 MINUTES)

Because of the widespread death of Egyptian firstborns, Pharaoh was compelled to let the Israelites go with Moses. As Pharaoh's sadness turned quickly to rage, he led an army of "six hundred chosen chariots . . . [with] captains over every one of them. . . . And he pursued after the children of Israel . . . and overtook them encamping by the sea."[104]

How terrified would you have been if you had been an Israelite? All you know is slavery, oppression, abuse, and death at the hands of the very people who have you trapped. Imagine all the trauma the Israelites felt having never experienced victory over the Egyptians for the past 430 years. This is why the testimony of prophets is invaluable, especially when we find ourselves in situations where we feel trapped and without hope.

Moses confidently testified, "Fear ye not, stand still, and see the salvation of the Lord, which he will shew to you to day: for the Egyptians whom ye have seen to day, ye shall see them again no more for ever. The Lord shall fight for you, and ye shall hold your peace."[105]

---

104 Exodus 14:5–9.
105 Exodus 14:13–14.

Please mark this testimony. If you use digital scriptures, open the toolbar, and click "Note." In this note, type a story about an experience when the Lord fought for you. If you use paper scriptures, write notes in the margins so you can remember a story of when the Lord fought for you. While pondering, watch this music video by Aberdeen Lane. As you watch, ask the Lord to help you remember and feel times when He has fought for you.

(Or google "I Stand All Amazed, Beautiful Savior, Amazing Grace by Aberdeen Lane")

WALLS (10 MINUTES)

Disclaimer: I am not a Hebrew scholar, so take this next part as simply an interesting word connection. One of the most popular images Isaiah conjured was when he responded to Zion's deep fear of the Lord forgetting them. Speaking Messianically (as if Isaiah were speaking the words of Christ), he testified, "Can a woman forget her sucking child, that she should not have compassion on the son of her womb? yea, they may forget, yet will I [Jesus] not forget thee." As if this image isn't powerful enough, he deepened the image in the next verse. "Behold, I have graven thee upon the palms of my hands; thy walls are continually before me."[106] I will discuss the deep meaning of Christ's feelings for us likened to a mother's feelings toward her vulnerable child when we study Isaiah 49 in September.

For our study this week, I want to point out the very last phrase of verse 16, "Thy walls are continually before me." The Savior is essentially promising us that He is with us, He knows what we go through, and He will never leave us completely alone. The Hebrew connection I want to make here is regarding the word *walls*. The word used in Hebrew is the feminine noun *chomah*. This is the same Hebrew word used in Exodus 14 regarding the parting of the Red Sea.

> And the children of Israel went into the midst of the sea upon the dry ground: and the waters were a *wall* unto them on their right hand, and on their left.[107]

> But the children of Israel walked upon dry land in the midst of the sea; and the waters were a *wall* unto them on their right hand, and on their left.[108]

It makes me wonder if during the time of Isaiah, the use of *chomah* would have reminded Isaiah's people of the miracle of the parting of the Red Sea. In addition to all the many principles we learn from the children of Israel's being delivered, does Isaiah also want us to learn that even when the children of Israel felt surrounded and forsaken by God and forgotten, Jesus *still* remembered them, was in their midst, and delivered them?

This principle is taught in Exodus and Isaiah, and it is taught in a scripture President Thomas S. Monson often quoted, "And whoso receiveth you, there I will be also, for I will go before your face. I will be on your right hand and on your left, and my Spirit shall be in your hearts, and mine angels round about you, to bear you up."[109] As the Israelites *passed over* (*passover)* the Red Sea and saw Pharaoh's army destroyed, I wonder how many

of them had the same testimony. Jesus was with them, on their right wall and left wall. He delivered them.

What are some things you would say to someone who feels like God has forsaken them? Do you have an experience you could share or a testimony you could bear? As you consider this scenario, watch the following music video by popular Christian singer Lauren Daigle.

(Or google "Lauren Daigle Rescue Official Music Video")

Write down your possible responses here:

_____

_____

_____

MUSIC IS WHAT FEELINGS SOUND LIKE (10 MINUTES+)

One day early in our marriage, I was loudly singing a song in the car. My wife, Paige, was not at all impressed. While we were laughing at how poor my musical talents were, I told her something like, "Wait until the resurrection. When I have resurrected vocal cords, I'm going to be an amazing singer!" Paige looked at me in disbelief and said, "I doubt it. I always assumed people who sing as bad as you won't sing in heaven either. I figured they would give you a horn to play or something like that." Shocked, I replied, "You don't think the power of the Resurrection of Jesus Christ can heal my terrible singing voice?" Without hesitation she responded, "Nope, I don't." Now we are both anticipating our resurrection just to see who is right.

In Exodus 15, Moses and the Israelites sing a "song unto the Lord."[110] Read the lyrics to their song in Exodus 15:1–21 and mark the lyrics you like. Assume each *verse* of the scripture is a *verse* of the song. If you are studying in a group, read these verses either alone or together. At the end, have each person share their favorite part, or *verse*, of the song.

---

106   Isaiah 49:15–16.

107   Exodus 14:22, emphasis added.

108   Exodus 14:29, emphasis added.

109   Doctrine and Covenants 84:88.

110   Exodus 15:1.

When you are done, listen to songs, hymns or otherwise, that praise the Lord. In the Church's *Hymnbook*, these are specifically hymns 62–96. If you are a musical family, you may want to sing some of these or play them on a musical instrument or both. This could be your study for the next few days. How has music been such an effective way to express your feelings? What songs help you connect and align with Christ? If you are like me, you may need some help in this area. Here are a couple of praise songs you can listen to.

These songs slap!

(or google "He Reigns, Strive to Be")

(or google "Amazing Grace (ft. Alex Boyé) The Five Strings")

(or google "Free My Soul, Youth Music Festival 2021")

(or google "How Great Thou Art Carrie Underwood Official Performance Video")

(or google "Alex Boyé—I Will Rise (Emi Yo Leke) ft. LDC")

FOOD (15 MINUTES)

If you could only eat one food for the rest of your life, what would it be? Now make it more interesting: go through your kitchen and pick one item you could eat every day for the rest of your life. I will grab the peanut butter M&Ms. Eat whatever food you grabbed as you watch these videos.

I am amazed at how the Lord can use such simple, daily items—like food—to teach us complex spiritual lessons that can legitimately change our lives. As you read the instructions of how the Israelites were to be fed manna from heaven in Exodus 16, watch the following videos where Elder D. Todd Christofferson shared principles and insights into our own personal journey of gathering daily manna. After each video, write down at least one highlight.

DAILY BREAD: PATTERN

(Gospel Library -> Videos and Images -> Inspirational Videos -> Daily Bread: Pattern)

Highlight:

_____

_____

_____

_____

_____

DAILY BREAD: EXPERIENCE

(Gospel Library -> Videos and Images -> Inspirational
Videos -> Daily Bread: Experience)

Highlight:

_____

_____

_____

_____

_____

DAILY BREAD: CHANGE

(Gospel Library -> Videos and Images -> Inspirational
Videos -> Daily Bread: Change)

Highlight:

_____

_____

_____

_____

_____

APRIL 11–17

"HE WILL SWALLOW UP DEATH IN VICTORY"

EASTER

God's Message to Me from This Section

OLD TESTAMENT OBJECT LESSONS (10 MINUTES)

During a BYU Devotional, Elder David A. Bednar asked, "What is the most valuable substance or commodity in the world?" Before you read his answer, what are your best three guesses?

1. _____

2. _____

3. _____

Elder Bednar continued:

> We might initially think that gold, oil, or diamonds have the greatest worth. But of all the minerals, metals, gems, and solvents found on and in the earth, the most valuable is water.
>
> Life springs from water. Life is sustained by water. Water is the medium required to perform the various functions associated with all known forms of life. Our physical bodies are approximately two-thirds water. Whereas a person can survive for many days or even weeks without food, an individual will usually die in only three or four days without water. Most of the world's great centers of population are situated near sources of fresh water. Simply stated, life could not exist without the availability of and access to adequate supplies of clean water.[111]

Have you noticed the central theme of water so far in the Old Testament? Water is interesting because it represents potential, both in cleansing and destroying. Water has the potential to nourish and sustain life, yet it also has the power to destroy it. For example, a river flowed through the Garden of Eden, sustaining life. Isaac and Jacob found their wives by wells of water. On the other hand, the earth was cleansed from evil by a destructive flood. In the story of the Exodus, the Red Sea brought both deliverance to the Israelites and death to the Egyptians. Can you think of other examples in the scriptures where water is used as an object lesson?

Blood is also deeply instructive in scripture. The Passover was first introduced to the Israelites in Egypt just before they were liberated. The final plague that compelled

111 "The Scriptures: A Reservoir of Living Water," BYU Speeches, February 4, 2007.

Pharaoh to release these people was the death of all Egyptian firstborns.[112] As you studied last week, the Israelites were invited to use the blood of a firstborn, unblemished lamb to mark their doors, ensuring the destroying angel would "passover" their homes and spare their children.[113]

It is important to recognize that the general masses in the Old Testament were illiterate. The 400-years-enslaved Israelites were no exception. They could not read! However, lessons of Jehovah's deliverance using water and blood would have been unmistakable to them. Here are some similarities between the Passover sacrifice and the atoning sacrifice of Jesus:[114]

Passover	Jesus
The firstborn male lamb	The Only Begotten Son, the Lamb of God
The blood of the lamb saved lives	The blood of the Lord purifies all who are faithful
No broken bones	The Lord suffered no broken bones in His death (see John 19:31–36)
Partake of unleavened bread (no yeast)	The bread of life. As we partake of Him (taking His name upon us), we can be purified
This bread couldn't spoil or mold	It symbolized a repentant and purified person
Partake in haste	Respond enthusiastically to the offer of the Lord

Take a few minutes today, and each day this week, to watch at least one video that centers on the delivering and redemptive power of Jesus Christ. The Church of Jesus Christ of Latter-day Saints has a video collection specifically for Easter that is extraordinary! After you watch each video, fill in the blank:

Because of Jesus Christ, _____

_____.

---

112 See Exodus 12.
113 See Exodus 12:3–7.
114 Ed J. Pinegar, Richard J. Allen, *Teachings and Commentaries of the Old Testament*, Covenant Communications (2005), 357.

Use the following QR code to find this collection:

(Gospel Library -> Videos and Images -> Holiday Videos -> Easter Videos)

THEIR STORY, YOUR STORY (10 MINUTES)

The story of the Exodus is the story of the plan of salvation. It is also your story! Read the story of the Israelites and then follow the prompts on the right to pattern your life's story in relation to the plan of salvation.

The Plan of Salvation	The Story of the Israelites	My Story
The Fall	Like the Israelites, we come to earth surrounded by the taskmasters of devils, sin, and human experience. Representing the effects of the Fall, we too gain knowledge and discover a deep need for deliverance and liberation. We stretch and seek as communities and individuals for divine help.	How have I experienced the Fall?
Prophets and Divine Guidance	Like Moses, prophets and seers are provided to: testify of Christ's delivering power provide much-needed guidance for us to follow invite us to seek a personal relationship with Christ.	Why are prophets valuable to me?

Redemption through Jesus Christ	As we choose to attach ourselves to Jesus Christ through covenants, we are choosing to attach ourselves to His redemptive power. Because of Him, we "passover" death and destruction through His blood and living water.	What has Jesus helped me "passover" in my life?
Faithfully Enduring to the End	Redemption almost never provides an instantaneous and immediate "happily ever after." Rather, redemption provides the expansive atoning power to *help* us in our mortal trials[115] and provides the promise of eternal life with our Heavenly Parents.	What motivates me to endure?
Promised Lands	As we faithfully and joyfully endure life's difficulties with Jesus Christ by our side, we will experience the future blessing of entering the promised land of eternal life.	What heavenly promises do you most look forward to?

---

115 See January 3–9 lesson.

APRIL 18–24
"ALL THAT THE LORD HATH SPOKEN WE WILL DO"
EXODUS 18–20

God's Message to Me from This Section

EXODUS 18:13–18—ICEBERGS (20 MINUTES)

Get a piece of paper and draw a big iceberg. What are some characteristics of icebergs? On average, only ten percent of the mass of an iceberg is visible above water. If you haven't already, draw the waterline of your iceberg so ninety percent of your drawing is below it.

Icebergs are a very simple teaching tool to help us understand ourselves and how to interact with others, or minister, in more useful ways. They are also useful in how we interact with ourselves. Assume the ten percent of what we can see represents our behaviors—*what* we do. Now assume that ninety percent of what we can't see in the dark water represents our beliefs and values that feed our behaviors—*why* we do what we do. Here's my amazing drawing:

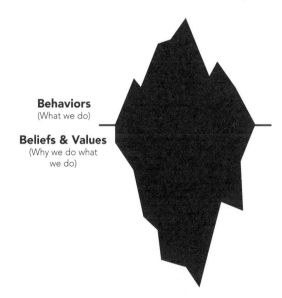

Behaviors
(What we do)

Beliefs & Values
(Why we do what we do)

From my observation as a life-long member of The Church of Jesus Christ of Latter-day Saints, we minister backward. We focus ninety percent of our energy on behavior and only ten percent on *why* we behave the way we do. To illustrate this, let's play a game with one of my favorite Church videos. Identify the hero(es) and the villain(s) in the video.

(Gospel Library -> Videos and Images -> Inspirational Messages -> Come unto Jesus)

(or google "Come unto Jesus, Madilyn Paige")

Okay, who were the heroes, and who was the villain? How could you tell?

Now watch the video again, and think about some possible reasons why the "villain" may have acted the way he did. What could be going on in his life that could trigger his angry behavior? When I do this in a seminary class, here are some student responses:

- Maybe he's been unemployed for a year. He was a finalist for a job and just found out someone else got it.

- Maybe he's coming home from the funeral of his spouse, a child, a parent, his best friend, etc.

- Maybe he was abused and finally reached out to get help from a close friend and the friend didn't believe him.

Of course, my purpose is not to excuse his rude behavior. My point is to not rush to judgment because you think you know what's really going on in his life based solely on his behavior. Let's fill in the iceberg with some compassionate assumptions:

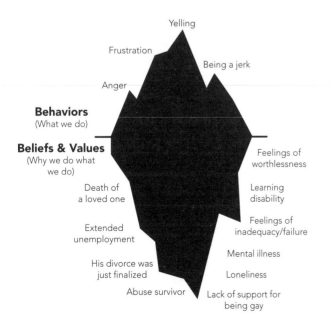

Go back to your original drawing and write down your own behaviors that aren't serving you. Write down what is going on in the dark water that is feeding these behaviors.

I took the long way to teach one verse because I think it's that important. In Exodus 18, the burden of leadership was crushing Moses. The people wanted Moses's help "from the morning unto the evening."[116] Jethro, Moses's father-in-law, noticed the extreme toll this was taking on Moses and asked, "What is this thing that thou doest to the people? why sittest thou thyself alone, and all the people stand by thee from morning unto even?" Moses explained, "The people come unto me to inquire of God. . . . And [Jethro] said unto him, The thing that thou doest is not good."[117] Pause right here and consider *why* Moses was participating in behavior that was "not good." In other words, consider what might be going on under the surface.

- Maybe Moses was doing this because he believed he was the only one who could judge the people correctly.[118]

- Maybe Moses wanted to do a really good job.

- Maybe Moses felt like he didn't have enough time to train anyone else.

- Maybe Moses was doing the very best he could and he was just not sure how to ask for help.

- Maybe Moses didn't want to fail his people or God.

Now we finally get to the one verse I wanted to emphasize: Jethro, ministering to Moses, probably knew exactly *why* Moses was struggling. He said, "Thou wilt surely wear away, both thou, and this people that is with thee: for this thing is too heavy for thee; thou art not able to perform it thyself alone."[119] Jethro continued to help Moses see a different way—there were many others who were already rulers. He instructed Moses to train them and allow them to help carry the burden of the people that it might be light.[120]

116 Verse 13.

117 Exodus 18:13–15,17.

118 "In Hebrew, the word translated as *judge* means more than a judiciary official. In the Hebrew tradition, 'to judge' means to lead and usually includes leading in political, judicial, military, and spiritual ways. This is how the term is used in the Old Testament and typically how it is also used in the Book of Mormon" (Kerry Muhlestein, "The Essential Old Testament Companion," [2013] Covenant Communications, 112).

119 Exodus 18:18.

120 It may be useful to reread our baptismal covenants in context of Jethro's example of master ministering. See Mosiah 18:8–10.

Ministering Lesson: It is much more effective to dive into the deep water of a person's life to better understand *why* they are behaving the way they are. If we are talking only about behavior, we will get only surface results. If we want deep change in behavior, we need to explore beliefs and values in deeper ways.

Next time you are in a situation to minister, put on your scuba gear and dive deep. Let the person know you're there for them, that you love them, and that you accept them. Can you think of an example from the life of Jesus Christ when He dove into the dark water of someone's life to help them? This brings a whole new meaning to the scriptures that teach us Jesus "descended below all things."[121]

Who do you know who is a Christ-like example of ministering? Is there something you can do to minister in a more useful way?

EXODUS 19—VENDING MACHINES & HEAVENLY BEINGS (15 MINUTES)

What is your favorite vending machine food and drink? When I was in middle school and high school, vending machines were my favorite. They're simple—you insert money, and in exchange, you get to choose whatever treat or drink you want.

This vending machine idea is *not* the kind of relationship God wants to have with us, yet sometimes we believe it's the way heaven works. God is not a *transactional* Being. He is a *relational* Being. A transactional relationship with God would mean we approach Him with our money, or good works, with the purpose of getting exactly what we want. Then we forget about the vending machine until the next time we want something. Viewing our good works as negotiation leverage to get whatever we want from God is not useful. A good example of the extreme effects of transactional discipleship is the Pharisees in the days of Jesus. Near the end of His ministry, Jesus gave the Pharisees this scathing rebuke: "Woe unto you, scribes and Pharisees, hypocrites! for ye are like unto whited sepulchres, which indeed appear beautiful outward, but are within full of dead men's bones, and of all uncleanness."[122]

The reason I bring this up is that in our *Come, Follow Me* studies, Moses is about to receive the Ten Commandments. Knowing *why* we keep commandments is just as important as keeping them. Choosing to keep God's commandments is choosing to allow His influence to prevail in our lives. Choosing to keep commandments is to practice living the type of lifestyle our Heavenly Parents live. Jesus taught this principle: "And this is life eternal, that they might know thee the only true God, and Jesus Christ, whom thou hast sent."[123] Keeping commandments is not so much about making a one-time payment as it is about investing, discovering our full divine potential over time, through experiences. And this becomes a relational partnership with God— we strive to live as He does because we love Him and want to be like Him, and because we make those efforts and draw closer to Him, He blesses us with what we want.

Elder Dallin H. Oaks gave this perspective and parable on *why* we should strive to keep commandments:

The Final Judgment is not just an evaluation of a sum total of good and evil acts—what we have *done*. It is an acknowledgment of the final effect of our acts and thoughts—what we have *become*. It is not enough for anyone just to go through the motions. The commandments, ordinances, and covenants of the gospel are not a list of deposits required to be made in some heavenly account. The gospel of Jesus Christ is a plan that shows us how to become what our Heavenly Father desires us to become.

A parable illustrates this understanding. A wealthy father knew that if he were to bestow his wealth upon a child who had not yet developed the needed wisdom and stature, the inheritance would probably be wasted. The father said to his child:

> All that I have I desire to give you—not only my wealth, but also my position and standing among men. That which I *have* I can easily give you, but that which I *am* you must obtain for yourself. You will qualify for your inheritance by learning what I have learned and by living as I have lived. I will give you the laws and principles by which I have acquired my wisdom and stature.

---

121 DC 122:8; 88:68; Genesis 28:12; 1 Nephi 11:30; Ephraim 4:7–11.

122 Matthew 23:27 (3–39).

123 John 17:3

Follow my example, mastering as I have mastered, and you will become as I am, and all that I have will be yours.[124]

Upon Mt. Sinai, the Lord gave Moses one example of why He hopes we choose to keep commandments: "Ye have seen what I did unto the Egyptians, and how I bare you on eagles' wings, and brought you unto myself. Now therefore, if ye will obey my voice indeed, and keep my covenant, then ye shall be a peculiar treasure unto me above all people: for all the earth is mine: And ye shall be unto me a kingdom of priests [and priestesses], and an holy nation. These are the words which thou shalt speak unto the children of Israel."[125]

What are at least three reasons for *why* you choose to keep the commandments that have deepened your relationship with Jesus and your Heavenly Parents?

1. _____

2. _____

3. _____

EXODUS 20—COMMANDMENTS = REVELATION (15 MINUTES)

I'm not exactly sure why, but I have always loved this video that provides observations, explanations, and clarity to the Ten Commandments. Watching this also reminds me how much I miss Elder L. Tom Perry.

(Gospel Library -> Videos and Images -> Inspirational Messages -> Obedience to the Ten Commandments)

(or google "Obedience to the Ten Commandments")

In the Doctrine and Covenants, almost every revelation includes commandments. The Doctrine and Covenants often uses the words *revelation* and *commandments*

interchangeably.[126] The scriptures mostly follow this same pattern. When Lehi received revelations, they included commandments to leave Jerusalem, to send his sons back for the plates, and to send them back again for Ishmael's daughters. Nephi's revelations were commandments as well: get the plates, follow the Liahona, build a ship, leave his abusive brothers, and build a temple. Joseph Smith received commandments to purify his heart; translate the golden plates; build a church; get baptized; baptize others; move to Ohio, then Missouri, and then Nauvoo; preach the gospel; teach truth; and build temples.

Don't be surprised if you are given a revelation from heaven in which you are commanded to "go and do" something hard.[127] We also learn from scripture that as we try to keep the commandments we will do so without fully knowing all the information about how or why.[128]

The difference between the commandments above and the Ten Commandments is that the commandments above were personalized to certain people at certain times. The Ten Commandments are universal and apply to all of us. If our Heavenly Parents want us to become like Them, the Ten Commandments are really just characteristics that provide Them with Their heavenly lifestyle, power, liberation, and influence. Interestingly, all of the Ten Commandments can be categorized under each of the two great commandments, which are to love God and love our neighbors as ourselves.[129]

Take the Ten Commandments found in Exodus 20:3–17, and categorize each one as either a commandment to primarily love God or a commandment to primarily love our neighbors and ourselves.

Thou shalt have no other Gods before me.		
Thou shalt make unto thee no idols.		

124 "The Challenge to Become," *Ensign*, November 2000, 32.
125 Exodus 19:4–6.
126 Try this by using the word *revelations* instead of *commandments* in Doctrine and Covenants 1:17–18, 24, 30–32, 37.
127 1 Nephi 3:7.
128 See 1 Nephi 4:6; 9:3–6; 18:3.
129 Matthew 22:37–40.

Thou shalt not take the name of the Lord thy God in vain.		
Remember the Sabbath day, to keep it holy.		
Honor your father and your mother.		
Thou shalt not kill.		
Thou shalt not commit adultery.		
Thou shalt not steal.		
Thou shalt not bear false witness against thy neighbor.		
Thou shalt not covet.		

Read the following quote as you think about what difference it makes if we choose to keep commandments because we love God, self, and others.

> How clearly the Savior spoke when He said that every other commandment hangs upon the principle of love. If we do not neglect the great laws—if we truly learn to love our Heavenly Father and our fellowman with all our heart, soul, and mind—all else will fall into place.
>
> The divine love of God turns ordinary acts into extraordinary service. Divine love is the motive that transports simple words into sacred scripture. Divine love is the factor that transforms reluctant compliance with God's commandments into blessed dedication and consecration.
>
> Love is the guiding light that illuminates the disciple's path and fills our daily walk with life, meaning, and wonder.
>
> Love is the measure of our faith, the inspiration for our obedience, and the true altitude of our discipleship.
>
> Love is the way of the disciple.[130]

130 Dieter F. Uchtdorf, "The Love of God," *Ensign*, November 2009, 24.

APRIL 25–MAY 1
"MY PRESENCE SHALL GO WITH THEE"
EXODUS 24; 31–34

God's Message to Me from This Section

EXODUS 24—THE MOST IMPORTANT PROPHETS (10 MINUTES)

In your opinion, who are the three most important prophets who ever lived? (You can't say Jesus.)

Here are some options to get you thinking: Adam, Enoch, Noah, Joseph of Egypt, Moses, Isaiah, Jeremiah, Elijah, Peter, Lehi, Nephi, Abinadi, King Benjamin, Alma, Alma the Younger, Samuel the Lamanite, the Brother of Jared, Mormon, Moroni, Joseph Smith, Russell M. Nelson.

Who did you choose? Is there actually a right answer to this question? I'm not sure if this fully answers that question, but Ezra Taft Benson taught, "The living prophet has the power of TNT. By that I mean 'Today's News Today.' God's revelations to Adam did not instruct Noah how to build the ark. Noah needed his own revelation. Therefore, the most important prophet, so far as you and I are concerned, is the one living in our day and age to whom the Lord is currently revealing His will for us."[131]

As Israel was beginning to accept the words of the Lord that Moses was teaching, the Lord revealed Himself to the seventy elders of Israel, Moses, and a few others. Exodus 24 is deeply relational and identifies the

personal relationships we receive by accepting and living according to heavenly covenants. In addition, Exodus identifies important attributes of prophets and the role they play in covenant making. See what you can find in the following verses:

- Exodus 24:1–2,12

_____

- Exodus 24:3

_____

- Exodus 24:4

_____

- Exodus 24:5

_____

- Exodus 24:7

_____

- Exodus 24:8

_____

- Exodus 24:10

_____

---

131 BYU Speeches, "Fourteen Fundamentals in Following the Prophet," February 26, 1980.

Which of these attributes of prophets do you have a deep testimony of? Which of these attributes of prophets do you want to understand better? Have you had an experience where following a prophet was important for you?

EXODUS 32–34—WHICH WAY DO YOU FACE? (10 MINUTES)

If you have a picture of the Savior in your home, please face the Savior as you begin reading Exodus 32. Jesus helped the Israelites face Him in the wilderness by liberating them from Egypt, parting the Red Sea, providing the miracle of daily manna from heaven, and giving them the Ten Commandments. But at this point, Moses had been on Mount Sinai for about forty days, and the Israelites didn't know what happened to him. Their worship then turned from God to another form of worship. As you read Exodus 32:1–6, slowly turn away from the Lord until you are facing the opposite direction, with your back to Him. Exodus 32:7–8 speaks directly to the new direction the Israelites were now facing.

Why was Aaron such a willing participant? Old Testament scholars D. Kelly Ogden and Andrew C. Skinner wrote:

> Aaron, whom Moses left in charge (Exodus 24:14–18), tried to rationalize that it was a "feast to the Lord" (Jehovah) whom they would celebrate by their offerings, their eating and drinking, and their "play" before the calf (vv. 5 and 6). It may have been Aaron's original intent to provide a visual image to try to turn the people's faith back to the true and living God, but we really do not know why Aaron acted as he did. It was certainly not wholly out of righteousness. *Apparently it was a far greater challenge to get Egypt out of Israel than to get Israel out of Egypt.*[132]

Can you think of some ways that you are tempted to turn away from the Savior and His divine directions?

Although Moses was very clear, the Israelites' behavior was still unacceptable, and the rest of the book of Exodus details what God commanded the children of Israel to

build so they would always remember which way they faced. In preparation for the tabernacle, Exodus 33–34 includes loving yet stern course corrections to help the people return to the Lord.

---

132 D. Kelly Ogden and Andrew C. Skinner, *Verse by Verse: The Old Testament*, 2 vols. [2013], 1:233–34 (emphasis added).

MAY 2–8
"HOLINESS TO THE LORD"
EXODUS 35–40; LEVITICUS 1; 16; 19

God's Message to Me from This Section

EXODUS 25–30 AND 35–40—TAKING THE MYSTERY AND SECRECY OUT OF THE TEMPLE (20 MINUTES)

One of the subjects youth ask me about most is temples. They wonder if they can learn anything to prepare themselves. They wonder why no one is willing to talk more openly about them. My first comment is, "Just because it's unfamiliar, it doesn't mean it's weird." For example, what if you have a friend who has never heard of baptism before and they ask you to describe it. You tell them that you dress in an all-white, one-piece jumper. You walk down some stairs into a small swimming pool full of warm water, where another person holds your hand. The pool is below the ground because it symbolizes the death of Christ. The other person says a prayer, and then you are completely dunked into the water and brought back up again, representing the death of your old life and your desire to have a new life in Christ. The whole thing takes about thirty seconds. Oh, and we do the same thing on behalf of our dead ancestors, except the small pool sits on the back of twelve oxen. Then our dead ancestors, who are in the spirit world, get to choose to accept this baptism or reject it.

Is it just me, or does baptism kind of sound weird in that context? Why don't we think baptism is weird? Because we are so familiar with it. My goal is to help

you become more familiar with the temple.

I have learned that just because we have made covenants not to share a few things, it *doesn't* mean we can't share anything. Before you report me to Church headquarters, let me explain by using the scriptures we all have access to! The scriptures, especially the Old Testament, teach temple symbolism in deep ways. So put a helmet on. Exodus 35–40 is about to blow your mind!

Exodus chapters 25–30 are the revelation of the tabernacle God gave to Moses on Mt. Sinai. Chapters 35–40 follow the actual building of the tabernacle, as led by Moses. Therefore, there is a *spiritual* creation first, then a *physical* creation of the tabernacle follows. This is a core principle of how the earth was created![133]

1. Please get out a piece of paper and draw the following, or if you study on your own, write directly on this page. Leave some room to write basic tabernacle/temple symbolism on your page.[134]

---

133 See Moses 3:5.
134 *Old Testament Seminary Teacher Manual*, "Lesson 52: Exodus 25–27" [2015], 30.

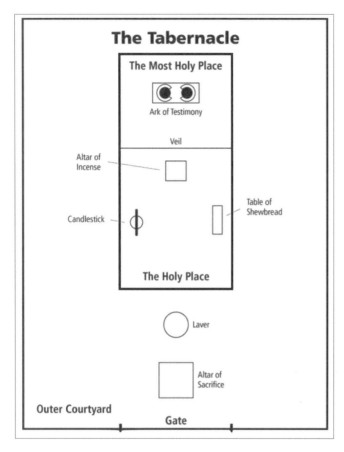

2. As you watch the following video, look for the many beautiful ways the temple symbolically teaches us about redemption through Jesus Christ, the plan of salvation, and why choosing a covenant path is worth it.

(or google "The Ancient Tabernacle and the Savior")

3. What symbolisms were most impactful to you? Write your insights next to the corresponding symbol on your drawing.

4. Here are some scripture references to the different elements of the tabernacle. Please add these references to your picture:

• Candlestick (with seven lamps): Exodus 25:31–32, 37–40; 26:35

• Table of shewbread: Exodus 25:23, 29–30; 26:35

• Altar of sacrifice: Exodus 27:1–8; 30:18

• Altar of incense: Exodus 30:1–8

• Laver (basin of water): Exodus 30:17–21

Did this lesson help take the mystery and secrecy out of the temple? I hope so.

EXODUS 35–40—THEIR EXPERIENCE, MY EXPERIENCE (20 MINUTES)

As you begin, take the following quiz to see if you can "name that temple."[135]

One of my favorite things to do when I want to deep dive into a gospel topic is to analyze it before I try to apply it. The more effectively I analyze, the more natural and powerful my application is. It is in the analysis that the Holy Spirit often whispers relevance. The most common way I analyze is to, the best I can, answer the question, "What did _____ mean to _____, then?" For example, in a previous lesson, I described the significance of the relationship between Laman and Nephi to describe the importance of the birthright during Old Testament times. Knowing what it meant to Laman to have all of Lehi's property stolen from them is an integral part of the story, especially since it was Nephi's idea.[136]

Before we make personal applications of the tabernacle, let's analyze:

"What did the tabernacle mean to the children of Israel, then?"

Here is an example of how to do this using a tabernacle diagram similar to the one at the beginning of this lesson. Try the best you can to put yourself in *their* shoes. Over the last 400 years, we and our ancestors have built significant, important structures for the Egyptians, many

---

135 "Name That Temple," posted Jan. 4, 2017, https://thirdhour.org/blog/quiz/easy/name-that-temple.
136 See lesson for Genesis 28–33.

of which represent who they worship and the power of the character being worshipped. Building structures is in our blood. As we work together, each person contributing to the overall project using their unique talents, what are we thinking about? What are we discussing? What is our excitement level? What spiritual experiences are we having? As we build the tabernacle, does it feel different than the Egyptian projects we've worked on? As we build, how do our Sabbath day conversations change?

Analyze this picture as if you were one of them. Use the questions above if it helps. Maybe pretend you are interviewing some of these people. What questions would you ask them? Don't move on too quickly. Analyze!

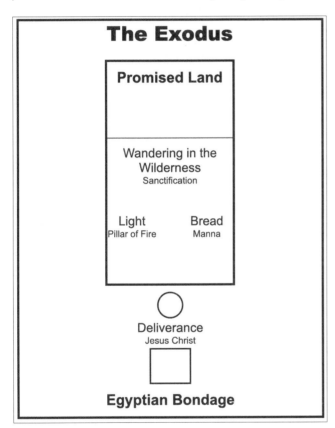

If I were one of them, what elements of my testimony would hopefully be strengthened as I participated in building the tabernacle?

- If Jesus Christ can deliver me from the power of Egypt, surely He can deliver me from anything else.

- Just because I have chosen to follow Christ by covenant, it does not mean I am now immune to wilderness experiences.

- There is divine purpose in my mortal wanderings.

- I am not left alone when I struggle. Through covenants, Jesus will lead me by the light of personal revelation and will help fill me with the bread of divine hope and trust.

- Jesus Christ sees me, is aware of my struggles, and has a divine plan to help me, my family, and all the children of our Heavenly Parents.

- What would you add? _____
_____
_____

Before we move to the final phase of personal relevance, let me briefly expand the scriptural definition of *divine deliverance*. In the past, I used to think divine deliverance was only accomplished if the afflictions I experienced went away. Although that can be true at times, deliverance is far more complicated. Elder Tad R. Callister taught three ways Jesus helps us when we are in afflictions. He said:

- Sometimes He removes the affliction.

- Sometimes He strengthens us to endure.

- Sometimes He gives us an eternal perspective to better understand their temporary nature.[137]

Can you feel personal application naturally distilling upon your soul "as the dews from heaven"?[138]

Here is the same diagram ready to be applied to you.

You may want to identify and write on the diagram regarding the following:

- What personal *bondage* experiences have I faced?

- How does knowing that Jesus Christ sacrificed and died for me bring me hope?

- What are some of the dark and difficult wilderness experiences I have been through?

- In what ways has the sacrament and the influence of the Holy Ghost helped sanctify me and lead me during my wilderness experiences?

- How does analyzing the symbolic nature of the temple point me to Christ so I want to have a relationship with Him?

137 "The Atonement of Jesus Christ," *Ensign*, May 2019.
138 See Doctrine and Covenants 121:45–46.

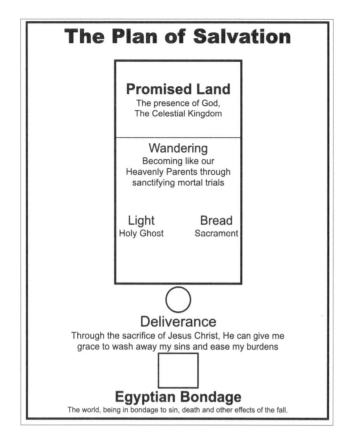

Take a couple of minutes to discuss how a basic Old Testament understanding of the tabernacle can help take the mystery and secrecy out of our modern temple worship.

LEVITICUS AND A COMEDIAN (10 MINUTES)

Have you ever started a *Come, Follow Me* lesson by watching a comedian? Today is your lucky day! For me, understanding and explaining Leviticus feels a lot like Nate Bargatze discussing the difficulty of time travel. Enjoy!

(or google "Nate Bargatze: Full Time Magic—Time Travel")

Leviticus is a very detailed book that describes how specific sacrifices for specific feasts should be accomplished.

In the detailed *procedures*, don't miss the deep *purposes*. "Ye shall be holy: for I the Lord your God am holy" (Leviticus 19:2; see also Leviticus 11:44–45; 20:26; 21:6).

In my own words, I would say, *Jesus Christ is not only willing but also capable of making us holy. Because of His character and saving power, we can attach ourselves to Him through the sanctifying power of sacrifice, repentance, and priesthood covenants.*

To help you better understand the feasts described in the Old Testament, scan the following QR code.

(Gospel Library -> Scriptures -> Study Helps -> Bible Dictionary -> Feasts)

MAY 9–15
"REBEL NOT YE AGAINST THE LORD, NEITHER FEAR"
NUMBERS 11–14; 20–24

God's Message to Me from This Section

NUMBERS 11–14; 20–24—HOW WELL DO YOU KNOW THE APOSTLES? (10 MINUTES)

Before you begin studying the book of Numbers this week, take this quiz to see how well you know the Apostles.[139]

"The book of Numbers describes some of what happened during those 40 years, including lessons the children of Israel needed to learn before entering the promised land. They learned about being faithful to the Lord's chosen servants (see Numbers 12). They learned about trusting the Lord's power, even when the future seems hopeless (see Numbers 13–14). And they learned that being faithless or untrusting brings spiritual harm, but they could repent and look to the Savior for healing (see Numbers 21:4–9)."[140]

---

139 "QUIZ: How Well Do You Know the Apostles?" posted Feb. 3, 2020, https://thirdhour.org/blog/quiz/quiz-do-you-know-apostles/.
140 "May 9–15 Numbers 11–14; 20–24," *Come, Follow Me—For Individuals and Families: Old Testament 2022,* ChurchofJesusChrist. org.

As the Lord used Moses to deliver Israel, restore ordinances, and create a culture of commandments and covenant keeping, He ran into a major problem—the people were relying too heavily upon Moses for divine help that they could receive on their own through personal revelation. In Numbers 11:4–6, the children of Israel were complaining about the continual expectation that they eat manna. They proclaimed, "Who shall give us flesh to eat? We remember the fish, which we did eat in Egypt freely; the cucumbers, and the melons, and the leeks, and the onions, and the garlick: But now our soul is dried away: there is nothing at all, beside this manna, before our eyes."

Can you think of a few things in our consistent church worship that we tend to overlook because it's so integrated into our lives?

One of my struggles is remembering how important the gift of the Holy Ghost is in my daily life. In a training for seminary and institute teachers, Elder David A. Bednar observed,

> As we honor our covenants, we may have the Holy Ghost as our constant companion. We often talk as if hearing the voice of the Lord through His Spirit is a rare event. *We should focus more on recognizing what happens to cause the*

Spirit to leave. If you and I are doing our best and not committing serious transgression, then we can always rely on the Holy Ghost to guide us.

Many people seem to believe that inspiration from the Holy Ghost is dramatic, big, and sudden. The truth is the Holy Ghost guides in still, small, and incremental ways over time. You often will not recognize that you are receiving revelation in the moment that you are receiving revelation.[141]

In this struggle, Moses laments, "I am not able to bear all this people alone, because it is too heavy for me." His solution? "Would God that all the Lord's people were prophets, and that the Lord would put his spirit upon them!" (Numbers 11:14, 29).

President Russell M. Nelson has taught us how and why personal revelation can bless our lives. Take a few minutes to brainstorm what you have learned from President Nelson about receiving revelation to guide your own life.

Can two people be confronted with the same situation and be inspired to handle it in totally different ways? Yes! Michelle D. Craig, former counselor in the Young Women General Presidency, taught,

> There are many ways to build the kingdom of God as covenant-making, covenant-keeping disciples of Jesus Christ. As His faithful disciple, you can receive personal inspiration and revelation, consistent with His commandments, that is tailored to you. You have unique missions and roles to perform in life and will be given unique guidance to fulfill them.
>
> Nephi, the brother of Jared, and even Moses all had a large body of water to cross—and each did it differently. Nephi worked "timbers of curious workmanship." The brother of Jared built barges that were "tight like unto a dish." And Moses "walked upon dry land in the midst of the sea."[142]

Use some of the following basic scenarios to analyze the importance of personal revelation. Also think about the many different ways the Lord could answer the questions people might have in these situations:

- Planning for adulthood (college, mission, job, etc.)
- Marriage (who, when, when not to, etc.)
- Children (when, when not to, how many, etc.)
- Retirement (when, when not to, what to do, etc.)

What other situations can you think of where many people can be confronted with the same situation but be led by the Spirit to manage them in completely different ways?

NUMBERS 21—HOW DO YOU KNOW WHAT SOMETHING IS WORTH? (15 MINUTES)

One way you can determine the worth of something is to look at the price that is paid for the item. This can be a meaningful lesson. Look around and identify three to five valuable objects in your home. Go through each item and ask what it is worth. See if others can guess the price that was paid for each item. Here are some examples:

- The newest phone is *worth* $1,000–$1,500. Why? Because that is the *price* people will pay for it.
- A video game console is *worth* $300–$600. Why? Because that is the *price* people will pay for it.

The real question is, What is the *worth* of a soul? Following the pattern above, the *worth* of a soul is determined by the *price* that was paid for the soul. Doctrine and Covenants 18:10 says, "The worth of souls is *great* in the sight of God."[143] This verse is beautiful, but it still doesn't answer the question. The answer to the question is in the next verse: "For, behold, the Lord your Redeemer suffered death in the flesh; wherefore he suffered the pain of all men, that all men might repent and come unto him."

The price that was paid for your soul and mine was the life and death of a God. If God paid an infinite price for your soul and mine, what does that say about the worth of souls? According to Jesus, His *infinite* sacrifice proves our *infinite* worth!

I bring this up now because you will read in Numbers 21 about the children of Israel being afflicted by fiery

---

141 "An Evening with Elder David A. Bednar," February 27, 2020 (emphasis added).
142 "Spiritual Capacity," *Ensign*, November 2019, 21.

143 Emphasis added.

(poisonous) serpents because of their constant complaining. "And the people spake against God, and against Moses, Wherefore have ye brought us up out of Egypt to die in the wilderness? for there is no bread, neither is there any water; and our soul loatheth this light bread" (Numbers 21:5).

Many of the children die, but many live. What saved them? And the Lord said unto Moses, "Make thee a fiery serpent, and set it upon a pole: and it shall come to pass, that every one that is bitten, when he looketh upon it, shall live" (Numbers 21:8)

The fiery serpent set on a pole is directly connected to the cross of Calvary. If the people will look to Christ for healing, they will be healed. The cross of Christ is a symbol we need to better understand. An empty cross represents both the love and life-giving power of Christ and testifies that we are all worth saving *if* we will choose to look to Christ.[144]

How do we choose to look to Christ? "And he hath risen again from the dead, that he might bring all men unto him, on conditions of repentance. And how great is his joy in the soul that repenteth!"[145] President Nelson similarly taught, "The Lord is gathering those who are willing to let God prevail in their lives. The Lord is gathering those who will choose to let God be the most important influence in their lives." He continued, "Are *you* willing to let God prevail in your life? Are *you* willing to let God be the most important influence in your life? Will you allow His words, His commandments, and His covenants to influence what you do each day? Will you allow His voice to take priority over any other? Are you

willing to let whatever He needs you to do take precedence over every other ambition? Are you *willing* to have your will swallowed up in His?"[146]

In my experience, really knowing through the power of the Holy Ghost that you are worth saving is one of the most important and influential testimonies you can have. That is what the cross teaches me. This testimony will limit shame, desperation, and rebellion. This testimony will bring hope, light, and life into situations that are unbearable. This truth will allow you to breathe, relax, and approach the gospel with confident curiosity.

CAMPING IS . . . (10 MINUTES)

When I was younger, my dad would take my brother and me camping in Montana for an entire week each summer. To this day, I still use the tent we slept in. We would fish, explore Yellowstone National Park, hike, cook, and laugh—a lot! As a teenager, I remember my brother and me racing to fall asleep before my dad because, let's just say, he wasn't the quietest sleeper. Sometimes I'd wake up in the middle of the night, startled, thinking a grizzly bear was in our camp. No, it was just Dad. (Sorry, Dad.)

My point is camping experiences, for better or worse, are usually memorable. For example, my brother was reeling in a massive rainbow trout and I had the net in the water, ready to bring it up to shore. Just before I could net the fish, I felt a painful tug on my right ear. As I fell back, I watched the fish swim out of sight. We all looked at each other, confused, wondering who was to blame. I grabbed my ear and realized that just before I could net the fish, my brother pulled the hook out of the fish's mouth. As it snapped back toward my brother, it embedded in my right earlobe and pulled me away! (Sorry, Ryan.)

Although it is not included in the *Come, Follow Me* lesson, I think it is important to notice how the Israelites were directed to set up camp.[147] The object lesson is clear: the Israelites needed to make Jehovah the center of their lives. Or in President Nelson's words, "The Lord

---

144 See Alma 33:19–23; Helaman 8:14–15; 1 Nephi 17:41; John 3:14–15.

145 See Doctrine and Covenants 18:12–13.

146 "Let God Prevail," *Ensign*, November 2020, 92, 94.

147 *Old Testament Seminary Teacher Manual*, "Lesson 61: Numbers 1–10" (2015). For specific tribe assignments, see Numbers 2:3, 9–10, 16, 18, 24–25. For Levite responsibilities, see Numbers 3:25–26; 3:29, 31; 3:36–37; 3:38.

is gathering those who are willing to let God prevail in their lives. The Lord is gathering those who will choose to let God be the most important influence in their lives."[148]

As you read the following quote from Elder Dieter F. Uchtdorf, think about how the Church is organized today to help us and others.

> The Lord organized the Church in a way that offers each member an opportunity for service, which, in turn, leads to personal spiritual growth. . . .

You may feel that there are others who are more capable or more experienced who could fulfill your callings and assignments better than you can, but the Lord gave you your responsibilities for a reason. There may be people and hearts only you can reach and touch. Perhaps no one else could do it in quite the same way.[149]

CAMP OF ISRAEL

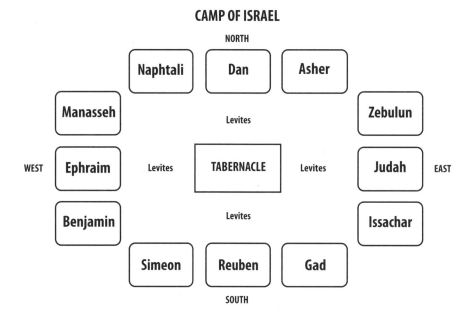

148 "Let God Prevail," *Ensign*, November 2020, 92, 94.

149 "Lift Where You Stand," *Ensign*, November 2008, 56. See also Numbers 4:49.

MAY 16–22
"BEWARE LEST THOU FORGET THE LORD"
DEUTERONOMY 6–8; 15; 18; 29–30; 34

God's Message to Me from This Section

DEUTERONOMY 6; 8; 29–30—WHO SAYS THE OLD TESTAMENT ISN'T ABOUT LOVE? (15 MINUTES)

The law of Moses is awesome! Growing up, however, I believed the law of Moses was a punishment reflected in a complicated gospel of checklists. I have often felt like the Old Testament's tone was, "Do this or else!" I believed they were so busy *doing* things, there was no room to *feel* anything.

Moses led the Israelites to the promised land but would be translated before he could enter the land with them.[150] Moses's role was to lead them out of Egypt and through the wilderness. Joshua's role was to lead them into the promised land and help build a community where God could be at the center of their lives. What is crucial for us to understand if we are to choose to put God at the center of our lives? Love!

In some ways, Deuteronomy is a kind of farewell from Moses to the children of Israel. As you read and mark the following verses, identify which ones impressed you most.

• Deuteronomy 6:4–7

• Deuteronomy 8:2–5

• Deuteronomy 8:11–17

• Deuteronomy 29:18–20

• Deuteronomy 30:6–10

• Deuteronomy 30:15–20

How powerful is knowing you are infinitely loved by your Parents in Heaven and Jesus Christ? The prophet Mormon was made the captain of the Nephite army at the age of fifteen! Throughout his life he experienced seventeen wars. It always surprises me that he is the prophet who teaches us that "charity suffereth long, and is kind, and envieth not, and is not puffed up, seeketh not her own, is not easily provoked, thinketh no evil, and rejoiceth not in iniquity but rejoiceth in the truth, beareth all things, believeth all things, hopeth all things, endureth all things.

"Wherefore, my beloved brethren, if ye have not charity, ye are nothing, for charity never faileth. Wherefore, cleave unto charity, which is the greatest of all, for all things must fail—

"But charity is the pure love of Christ, and it endureth forever; and whoso is found possessed of it at the last day, it shall be well with him."[151]

---

150 JST—Deuteronomy 34:6 clarifies, "For the Lord took him unto his fathers . . . therefore no man knoweth of his sepulchre unto this day." See also Alma 45:19.

151 Moroni 7:45–47.

Elder Uchtdorf explained,

> In my life, I lived through World War II. I lived through a divided Germany. I was a refugee twice. But throughout all of that, I relied on my firm belief that there is a God in heaven, there is a Jesus Christ, there is a Holy Ghost, and there is a restored gospel of Jesus Christ.
>
> My most personal experiences with hearing the Lord's voice have come when I think about how much I love the Savior and, in turn, feel His love for me. This love creates a connection—it opens a door—that allows me to feel the power of the Holy Ghost.[152]

Watch the following video and notice the role of love in Elder Uchtdorf's relationship with God and others.

(or google "How I #HearHim Elder Dieter F. Uchtdorf")

Both Mormon and Elder Uchtdorf grew up amid extreme human hatred. Wouldn't they be justified in hating their fellow humans? Yet they are two improbable examples of the power of love.

Go back to the scripture that impressed you the most from the previous list in this section and write it down. Keep it with you all week. Maybe you can even memorize some of it. You could take a picture of it and make it the wallpaper on your phone. What difference did it make during the week to be reminded consistently of love?

---

152 "HowIHearHim,"https://www.churchofjesuschrist.org/study/ manual/hear-him-launch/how-i-hear-him-uchtdorf?lang=eng.

DEUTERONOMY 15:1–7—WE TAKE CARE OF EACH OTHER (10 MINUTES)

Take a few minutes to find a video that inspires you to reach out in love to someone else. It does not need to be a Church-produced video. Here is one if you need some help:

(Gospel Library -> Videos and Images -> Inspirational Messages -> One in Christ)

(or google "Ulisses Soares One in Christ")

Read Deuteronomy 15:1–7 and mark the phrases that remind us to help each other. Now set a goal to help someone else this week. Pray each day and ask God to help you.

DEUTERONOMY 6; 8—LET'S DO SOME MATH! (10 MINUTES)

Is *scripture* >, <, or = *temptation*?

Deuteronomy + Jesus = the answer!

President Marion G. Romney of the First Presidency taught:

> [Jesus's] thorough knowledge of the scriptures is evidenced by the fact that He repeatedly cited them. When the devil tempted Him to turn the stones into bread, He countered by quoting from Deuteronomy:
>
> "It is written, Man shall not live by bread alone, but by every word that proceedeth out of the mouth of God" (Matthew 4:4; see Deuteronomy 8:3).
>
> When the tempter challenged Him to cast Himself down from the pinnacle of the temple, He responded by quoting from the same book:

"It is written again, Thou shalt not tempt the Lord thy God" (Matthew 4:7; see Deuteronomy 6:16).

For the third time He quoted from Deuteronomy (6:13) when Satan offered Him the kingdoms of the world, saying:

"Get thee hence, Satan: for it is written, Thou shalt worship the Lord thy God, and him only shalt thou serve" (Matthew 4:10).[153]

Brainstorm scriptures that you have relied on to get you through hard times. List them here:

_____

_____

_____

_____

_____

_____

_____

Now think of a temptation you are currently dealing with. Is there a scripture you came up with that could help you with this struggle? A constant temptation I have is to give up and stop trying. The scripture that has helped me a lot with this is: "Now ye may suppose that this is foolishness in me; but behold I say unto you, that by small and simple things are great things brought to pass; and small means in many instances doth confound the wise" (Alma 37:6). Here is a simple example. When I need to load the dishwasher and there is a mountain of dirty dishes to be cleaned, my first thought is to give up, ignore it, and hope someone else does it. When I approach Alma 37:6, my perspective changes. Instead of an insurmountable pile of dishes, I view the task as cleaning one dish. That, I can do! Then I do it again and again and again. A few minutes later, the task is done!

---

153 "Jesus Christ, Man's Great Exemplar," (address to Brigham Young University student body, May 9, 1967), 9.

MAY 23–29
"BE STRONG AND OF A GOOD COURAGE"
JOSHUA 1–8; 23–24

God's Message to Me from This Section

One common theme in the book of Joshua is no matter how great the obstacle, God can overcome it for us. One of His attributes is that He is a perfect problem solver. As you study the book of Joshua, notice the different ways we learn to trust in God's problem-solving power.

JOSHUA 1:8–9—PROBLEM SOLVING THROUGH SCRIPTURE (5 MINUTES)

This book of the law shall not depart out of thy mouth; but thou shalt meditate therein day and night, that thou mayest observe to do according to all that is written therein: for then thou shalt make thy way prosperous, and then thou shalt have good success.

Have not I commanded thee? Be strong and of a good courage; be not afraid, neither be thou dismayed: for the Lord thy God is with thee whithersoever thou goest.

Is there a specific scripture or scripture story that has helped you as you've faced a difficult problem? What story from your study of the Old Testament this year has been most useful for you?

A number of years ago, I lost my job. It took six months to find employment again. As many of you know, unemployment can be a massive obstacle physically, emotionally, and spiritually. During my mission, my mission president always testified that the Book of Mormon can help you with any obstacle you will ever face. But what about unemployment? There's *no* way the Book of Mormon could address unemployment, right? I started at 1 Nephi 1 and began to read with the question, "How can the Book of Mormon get me a job?" It wasn't long before I read 1 Nephi 16. This is the chapter where Nephi broke his bow. The impression came, "Nephi just lost the ability to provide for his family. Isn't that what you're feeling?" Studying this chapter over and over again for the next few days, I found many principles that could help someone who is unemployed.

Additionally, this chapter begins with the heavenly gift of the Liahona. As Lehi's and Ishmael's families travel through the wilderness, the Liahona is evidence that "God [was] with [them] withersoever [they went]."

Now I have a burning testimony that 1 Nephi 16 is the chapter for the unemployed. For me, it is a much-needed fulfillment of Joshua 1:8–9.

JOSHUA 3:13–17—PROBLEM SOLVING BY GETTING YOUR FEET WET (10 MINUTES)

Elder David A. Bednar taught:

> Recall how the Israelites came to the river Jordan and were promised the waters would part, and they would be able to cross over on dry ground. Interestingly, the waters did not part as the children of Israel stood on the banks of the river waiting for something to happen; rather, the soles of their feet were wet before the water parted. The faith of the Israelites was manifested in the fact that they walked into the water *before* it parted. . . . True faith is focused in and on the Lord Jesus Christ and always leads to action.[154]

What are some of the actions you take because you have faith in Jesus Christ? If you were giving a talk in sacrament meeting about Joshua 3:13–17, what personal story would you share?

JOSHUA 24:15—PROBLEM SOLVING USING AGENCY (5 MINUTES)

It is clear that Joshua and his family were committed to choosing Christ. But what does this mean? Were they committed to blind compliance? Were they committed because they were afraid of being punished? Were they committed because they wanted power over others? No, they were committed to let God prevail in their lives because they understood the eternal beauty of the enabling power of the Atonement of Christ.

As you watch the following video, think about how understanding the enabling power of Christ can motivate you to choose Him.

(or google "Inspiring Short: In the Strength of the Lord, David A. Bednar")

PROBLEM SOLVING TAKES TIME (20 MINUTES)

The book of Joshua teaches us that God is the perfect problem solver. We have discussed how God helps us solve problems by:

- Giving us scripture stories
- Inviting us to get our feet wet
- Providing His enabling power

Elder Peter Johnson of the Quorum of the Seventy is fascinating for a number of reasons. Many members of The Church of Jesus Christ of Latter-day Saints know him as the first African-American General Authority called in this dispensation. The following video shares his life's journey. He had to overcome many obstacles to find Christ. As you watch this video, see if you can identify some of the principles you learned studying the book of Joshua.

(or google "Running Toward the Light, Peter Johnson")

---

154 "Seek Learning by Faith," from a satellite broadcast address to Church Educational System educators, given on February 3, 2006. See also *Ensign*, September 2007, 63.

MAY 30–JUNE 5
"THE LORD RAISED UP A DELIVERER"
JUDGES 2–4; 6–8; 13–16

God's Message to Me from This Section

The general tone of the book of Judges is similar to the pride cycle highlighted specifically in Helaman in the Book of Mormon. This mindset will help you recognize important patterns and key principles that will make this book much more real in how you apply what is shared.

"The book of Judges recounts the history of the children of Israel from the time they settled in the land of Canaan after Joshua's death to the birth of Samuel (approximately 1400–1000 B.C.). . . .

"The book of Judges is named for the various rulers, called 'judges' (Judges 2:16–19), who are the book's central figures. These judges were generally military leaders and fighters more than preachers of righteousness."[155] The book of Ruth also fits within the timeline of Judges.

JUDGES 1–5—THE ENDOWMENT PATTERN (10 MINUTES)

The temple endowment is not nearly as foreign or hard to find in the scriptures as we sometimes think. It is everywhere in scripture—especially in the pride cycle. Simply look for stories of creation, knowledge of good and evil, different ways of experiencing the fall, and deliverance through a covenant relationship with Jesus

Christ. When this pattern becomes clear, you will see the endowment pattern all over the scriptures. When we discussed the tabernacle built in Moses's day, I highlighted this same pattern. Another example is in the very first verse of the Book of Mormon: Nephi introduced himself by identifying the endowment pattern in his life!

Endowment Pattern	The Life of Nephi (1 Nephi 1:1)
Creation	"I, Nephi, having been born of goodly parents"
Knowledge of good and evil	"I was taught somewhat in all the learning of my father"
Fall	"and having seen many afflictions in the course of my days"
Acceptance of the Atonement of Christ by covenant	"having been highly favored of the Lord in all my days"
Receiving further light and knowledge	"having had a great knowledge of the goodness and the mysteries of God"

---

155 *Old Testament Seminary Teacher Manual*, "Introduction to the Book of Judges," Church Educational System manual, 2015.

Now consider the pattern experienced in the first few chapters of the book of Judges. If you are struggling to see this pattern in scripture, simply look for the pattern of *Creation*, *Fall*, and *Atonement*.

Endowment Pattern	Judges 1–5
Creation	• The Israelites conquered Canaan and began to create their own civilization in Canaan and the surrounding lands (Judges 1)[156]
Fall (learning through experiencing both good and evil)	• The people served the Lord (Judges 2:7) • A later generation arose, "which knew not the Lord, nor yet the works which he had done in Israel" (Judges 2:10–12) • They did evil in the sight of God (Judges 4:1) • The Lord could no longer protect them so they were ruled by an enemy nation (Judges 4:2) • The Israelites cried to God for deliverance because they were oppressed for twenty years (Judges 4:3)
Atonement	• God heard their cries and lovingly provided Deborah, a prophetess and judge, to deliver them (Judges 4:4) • The Israelites were finally liberated, and "the land had rest forty years" (Judges 5:31)

The word *rest* in scripture means "the enjoyment of peace and freedom from worry and turmoil. The Lord has promised such rest to His faithful followers *during this life*. He has also prepared a place of rest for them *in the next life*."[157]

Notice this rest is experienced both in the present and in the future. In mortality, of course, we will feel only portions of this rest. The fulness of rest will not be experienced until after this life. Use the following questions to analyze your experiences with rest.

• When have I experienced a portion of "the enjoyment of peace and freedom from worry and turmoil . . . *during this life*," even if it was only for a short time?
• As I look forward to experiencing a fulness of "the enjoyment of peace and freedom from worry and turmoil . . . *in the next life*," what does that look like to me?

JUDGES 4:4; 5:7—LESSONS LEARNED FROM DEBORAH—JUDGE, PROPHETESS, MOTHER (15 MINUTES)

Deborah is a remarkable woman to study. In Hebrew, her name means "bee." Deborah's influence is characterized by three main roles: judge, prophetess, and mother in Israel. Read Judges 4:4 and 5:7 to mark these three titles.

Old Testament scholar Camille Fronk Olson described these roles further by explaining:

> As an exception to traditional roles, Deborah held and manifested unique titles and attributes, three of which are described in the book of Judges. First, she was the only woman in a long list of judges to rule Israel before the monarchy. Second, she was the only judge named in the book of Judges who also held the title of prophet, although no scriptural background explains her rise to prominence or her gift of prophetic wisdom. Finally, her appellation as a mother in Israel appears in a context that is unrelated to traditional motherhood and lacks evidence that she bore children. Deborah was a 'mother in Israel' not because she gave birth to a child but because she reared up Israel and led them back to the Lord. Collectively, these roles prepared her to become a heroine and example of effective, female leadership both to her contemporaries and to us. As a tool in the Redeemer's

156 As the Israelites were commanded to conquer lands, I used to wrongly assume that God didn't given these civilizations a chance before the Israelites overtook them. It turns out Laman and Lemuel had these same assumptions, which Nephi corrected (see 1 Nephi 17:32–33; 2 Nephi 25:9; Amos 3:7).
157 Guide to the Scriptures, LDS Gospel Library, "Rest"; emphasis added.

hand, Deborah bore witness that the Savior is the true Deliverer.[158]

DEBORAH'S LEADERSHIP AS A JUDGE

Judges in Israel at this time often led in military, religious, political, and judiciary matters. Today, women also take important leadership roles in business and other organizations. What are some ways women have positively influenced each of these groups? What other leadership roles are important for women to hold?

DEBORAH'S LEADERSHIP AS A PROPHETESS

A key characteristic of prophets is that they bring others to Jesus Christ. Deborah was no exception (see Judges 4:9,14; 5:1–5). Her faith in Jesus Christ was manifest in her willingness to deliver others to Him for their ultimate deliverance. Who do you know who is like a prophetess? Which women do you look to as spiritual leaders who deliver you to Christ?

DEBORAH'S LEADERSHIP AS A MOTHER

As Camille Fronk Olson pointed out, the evidence that defined Deborah as a "mother in Israel" does not mean she bore children. She bore Israel. To *bear* means "to carry the weight, support, or endure difficulty with." In other words, she helped the people in her community become their best selves. What women do you look to in your community who have an important, positive influence?

Deborah *leads*, *delivers*, and *bears* Israel in nontraditional female ways. Use the following boxes to brainstorm both traditional and nontraditional ways women lead, deliver, and bear today.

> **LEAD**

> **DELIVER**

> **BEAR**

THE VALUE OF FEMALE VOICES (20 MINUTES)

A significant issue many women have experienced historically is the inability to speak and have their voices heard. For reasons that are unclear in the text, Deborah's influence is directly attributed both to her opportunities to lead and to her voice being received as authoritative. To identify the depth of this issue, *Y Magazine* published a research article titled "When Women Don't Speak." The article also defines why women's influence is important, and it includes useful tools to create a Church culture of positive influence for both women and men. Here is one paragraph that caused me to analyze and reconsider how I interact at church: "Rather than outright misogyny, [BYU political-science professor Jessica R. Preece] says it's usually cultural norms and gendered messages that subtly—and profoundly—shape the rules of engagement. Individuals who suppress female speech may do so unwittingly. 'They may love women,' says Preece. 'They may even be a woman!' But as a society we have been 'slowly socialized over years to discount' female expertise and perspectives. The problem, in part, could be you. Preece says, 'We have lots of learning and unlearning to do.'"[159]

---

158 Camille Fronk Olson, *Women of the Old Testament* (Deseret Book Company [2009]), 107. (See pgs. 107–125 for a deeper exploration of the influence and character of Deborah.)

159 Brittany Karford Rogers, "Why Women Don't Speak," *Y Magazine,* Spring Issue 2020, magazine.byu.edu.

Please scan the following QR code and take the time to read the rest of the article this week. Look for what you learned and what you need to unlearn.

JUNE 6–12

"MY HEART REJOICETH IN THE LORD"

RUTH; 1 SAMUEL 1–3

God's Message to Me from This Section

After five months of attempting to draw *new* strength from the *Old* Testament, pause this week to take inventory on how things are going. It is more helpful if you approach this week with curiosity and observation rather than judgment and shame. My purpose is to help refocus your aim and provide hope as you look forward to the next few months of *Come, Follow Me*.

The content below is provided to help you observe where you are and then continue what is working and make adjustments as you feel inspired; this will help you move forward with faith. The characters in Ruth and 1 Samuel 1–3 are all continually doing this as they face unanticipated hardships. I call this dynamic discipleship. Ruth, Naomi, and Hannah are especially good examples of dynamic discipleship. Their examples are very inspiring!

PAPER AIRPLANES (15 MINUTES)

This is one of my favorite activities to do in class because it has so many applications, and it's super fun! If you study with a group, have one person read the following directions first to lead the activity. The principle you are teaching is *approaching the scriptures with the right focus will make a considerable difference in how the scriptures connect us to Christ*. Now to the airplane activity.

1. Give everyone a piece of paper and tell them they have ninety seconds to write their name on the paper somewhere, make a paper airplane, and throw

it. The person with the best airplane wins a prize (candy, a snack, a trip to Hawaii, etc.). Ready, set, GO! (If anyone asks for clarification on the ultimate goal, just tell them they need to make the best airplane.)

2. The leader constantly reminds the group of how much time they have left and encourages them to hurry. You could use dialogue such as, "It's already been thirty seconds. You better hurry!" Or, "There are only twenty-five seconds left; get ready!" The point is to purposely create a rushed atmosphere.

3. "5 . . . 4 . . . 3 . . . 2 . . . 1 . . . throw!"

4. Watch as the chaos culminates in everyone desperately throwing their airplanes in all directions. When I do this with groups, it's always fun to take a minute to collectively laugh at how bad some of their airplanes turned out.

5. Soon the group will intently wonder who won. The leader then asks, "Who do you think?" If it hasn't already, it will dawn on the group that they weren't exactly sure what it meant to make the "best airplane." The leader can pick any arbitrary spot in the room, and whichever airplane is closest to that spot wins. I usually pick my right shoe, a specific wall, or some other object. Present the award to the winner. Don't be surprised if everyone else is confused, disconnected, and unfulfilled.

What is the correct sequence of these words? AIM, FIRE, READY (The correct sequence is READY, AIM, FIRE.) What sequence of these words did we use in this activity? (READY, FIRE, AIM.)

When we study our scriptures, too often we take the READY, FIRE, AIM approach, especially in studying the Old Testament over the last five months. We can get caught up in so many unimportant details. If we have no real aim or purpose, we will find ourselves similarly frustrated, disconnected, and unfulfilled with our scripture study.

The principle: *approaching the scriptures with the right focus will make a considerable difference in how the scriptures connect us to Christ.*

The next obvious question is, Are some truths in the scriptures more important than others? Elder Neal A. Maxwell taught, "All knowledge is not of equal significance. There is no democracy of facts! They are not of equal importance. Something might be factual, but not be important. For instance, today I wear a dark blue suit. That is true, but it is unimportant. As, more and more, we brush against truth, we sense that it has a hierarchy of importance. Some truths are salvationally significant and others are not."[160]

Finally, discuss the most important truths we can focus on to maximize the usefulness of our scripture study. Answers may vary to some degree, so here are some ways I would answer this.

The aim, or purpose, of scripture study in my home this week is . . .

- To find connection points to Jesus Christ.
- To deepen my relationship with God, self, and others.
- To give us strength to live our covenants through the grace of Jesus Christ.
- To build relationships with each other and with Christ.
- To better understand why Jesus Christ is worth worshipping.
- To allow time to turn down the noise of life and intentionally attempt to hear Him.

- To find common feelings with ancient disciples of Christ and learn wisdom from them as to how I can put Christ more at the center of my life.
- To become more like Christ in my tolerance of others, my willingness to listen without judgment, my ability to build up instead of tear down, and my desire to be an instrument in His hands to help others feel seen, noticed, and important.
- To feel a little bit more hope this week.

If you prefer, your aim, or purpose, could be to answer core questions. Here are the statements above in question form.

As I read the Old Testament this week . . .

- How could I use this story to connect with Jesus Christ?
- In what ways can I deepen my relationship with God, myself, and others?
- Where can I see Jesus Christ trying to help strengthen others? Where can I see His covenant grace in my day?
- How can I better connect with others and with Christ?
- Why is Jesus Christ worth worshipping?
- What difference does it make in my life to turn down the noise of life and intentionally attempt to hear Him?
- What common feelings do I share with these ancient disciples? What wisdom can I learn from them as I try to put Christ more at the center of my life?
- How can I be more tolerant of others, more willing to listen without judgment, more able to build up instead of tear down, and more desirous to be an instrument in His hands to help others feel seen, noticed, and important?
- In what ways can I feel a bit more hope this week?

Finalize this activity by writing down one to three ways that will help you *aim* your *Come, Follow Me* study for the next few months. For the next few weeks, it would be helpful to read these statements or questions before and after each study.

- _____

---

160 "The Inexhaustible Gospel," *Ensign*, April 1993; adapted from an address given 18 August 1992 at Education Week, Brigham Young University, Provo, Utah.

- _____

- _____

RUTH; 1 SAMUEL 1–3—FINDING CHRIST IN THE LIVES OF OTHERS (20 MINUTES)

The content below is meant to help you see different attributes of Jesus Christ in some of the main characters of Ruth and 1 Samuel 1–3. Use the statements and questions you defined above to analyze these characters with your specific *aim*. My hope is that the Holy Ghost will work with you to provide personalized messages.

"In the Old Testament, [Ruth is] the Moabite daughter-in-law of Naomi and Elimelech, who were Israelites. After the death of her husband, Ruth married Naomi's kinsman Boaz. Their son Obed was the ancestor of David and Christ. The story of Ruth beautifully illustrates the conversion of a non-Israelite into the fold of Israel. Ruth gave up her former god and former life to unite with the household of faith in serving the God of Israel (Ruth 1:16)."[161]

HOW IS RUTH LIKE ME?

A common pattern in the Bible is to symbolically refer to the Church as the bride and Jesus as the Bridegroom. John the Revelator testified, "I will shew thee the bride, the Lamb's wife" (Revelation 21:9). This pattern is embedded in the core of the book of Ruth. Ruth represents all who want God to prevail in their lives. Ruth represents you and me and our fallen need for help.

HOW IS RUTH LIKE CHRIST?

"Ruth's decision to take care of Naomi means that Ruth will eventually be left old and childless. In essence, Ruth is volunteering to take Naomi's suffering upon herself so that Naomi would not have to go through the suffering herself. In this way she becomes a symbol of the Savior, who suffered for us so that we will not have to."[162]

HOW ARE RUTH AND BOAZ LIKE ME AND JESUS?

When we study the book of Ruth this year, we may see a tender story of loss and loyalty. Or, considering this hierarchy of truth, we may notice that Ruth had lost her husband, that she journeyed to Bethlehem, and it was in Bethlehem where she met Boaz. We might then note that Boaz tended to Ruth's needs, gave her bread and a cup of wine vinegar, became her intercessor at the city's gate, and then, as her kinsman, which is literally translated "redeemer," purchased Ruth, took her to be his wife, and would not rest until he could say, "It is finished." With that we may begin to feel the intended testimony of love and redemption as well as the edification and inspiration from realizing that the Great Kinsman does the same for each of us.[163]

HOW IS HANNAH LIKE ME?

HOW IS HANNAH LIKE CHRIST?

WHAT ARE SOME THINGS I CAN LEARN ABOUT HOW TO *HEAR HIM* FROM SAMUEL?

161 Guide to the Scriptures, LDS Gospel Library, "Ruth."
162 Kerry Muhlestein, *The Essential Old Testament Companion* (Covenant Communications, [2013]), 199.
163 R. Kelly Haws, "First Seek to Obtain My Word," Seminaries and Institutes of Religion Satellite Broadcast, August 4, 2015. (See scripture references Ruth 1:19; Ruth 2:14; Ruth 4:1; Ruth 4:10; Ruth 4:13; see also Ruth 4 chapter heading; John 19:30; Ruth 3:18.)

JUNE 13–19
"THE BATTLE IS THE LORD'S"
1 SAMUEL 8–10; 13; 15–18

God's Message to Me from This Section

---

1 SAMUEL 8—THE "SAMUEL PRINCIPLE" (5 MINUTES)

In 1974, Ezra Taft Benson taught:

> If you see some individual in the Church doing things which disturb you, or you feel the Church is not doing things the way you think they could or should be done, the following principles might be helpful.

> God has to work through mortals of varying degrees of spiritual progress. Sometimes he temporarily grants to men their unwise requests in order that they might learn from their own sad experiences. Some refer to this as the "Samuel principle." The children of Israel wanted a king, like all the nations. The prophet Samuel was displeased and prayed to the Lord about it. The Lord responded by saying to Samuel, "They have not rejected thee, but they have rejected me, that I should not reign over them." The Lord told Samuel to warn the people of the consequences if they had a king. Samuel gave them the warning, but they still insisted on their king. So God gave them a king and let them suffer.

> They learned the hard way. God wanted it to be otherwise, but within certain bounds he grants unto men according to their desires. Bad experiences are an expensive school that only fools keep going to (see 1 Samuel 8).[164]

Think about the story of when Joseph Smith finally allowed Martin Harris to take the 116 manuscript pages. If you want a change of pace, read *Saints*, 1:49–53. Notice the "Samuel principle" at work in this experience. Rather than condemning Joseph for not listening to the Lord, consider what important lessons Joseph knew after this early life experience that would have been valuable later in life.

Has the Lord ever dealt with you or someone close to you in this way? Although the experiences were sad and brought great suffering, what value has come to you because of those difficulties?

1 SAMUEL 9; 16—THE DANGER OF RELYING *ONLY* ON MORTAL SIGHT (10 MINUTES)

Before you begin to study, find two containers. Try to find one container decorated on the outside and one that is much plainer. In the *more attractive* container,

---

164 "Jesus Christ—Gifts and Expectations," BYU Speeches, December 10, 1974.

put a less valuable item. In the *less attractive* container, put something much more valuable. Let your group know that one of the containers has something valuable in it. Without knowing what is inside each container, which would each person choose and why? This is a really fun activity to do in Primary and with youth. 1 Samuel 9 and 16 are about the dangers of making judgments based solely on outward appearances. Don't open the containers yet. Set them aside for later.

The king that Israel was hoping for turned out to be Saul. Saul is described as "a choice young man, and a goodly: and there was not among the children of Israel a goodlier person than he: from his shoulders and upward he was higher than any of the people" (1 Samuel 9:2). If the description of Saul sounds familiar, it's probably because you are thinking of Nephi (see 1 Nephi 2:16). However, Hebrew scholar Robert Altar observed, "Saul's looming size, together with his good looks, seems to be an outward token of his capacity for leadership, but as the story unfolds with David displacing Saul, his physical stature becomes associated with a basic human misperception of what constitutes fitness to command."[165]

Notice that the description of Saul is heavily based on outward appearance, even attributes Saul himself had little to no control over: youth and good looks. Have you ever misjudged someone because of their outward appearance?

In chapter 15, the Lord rejects Saul's leadership, and the prophet Samuel is commanded to seek out a new leader. Read 1 Samuel 16:1–7 and identify how the Lord sees His children. Bring back the containers and ask your group which container they would choose based on what they've learned so far.

The Lord expects us to make righteous judgments, but how? Read the following paragraph and identify the three key principles of righteous judgment.

"Our righteous judgments about others can provide needed guidance for them and, in some cases, protection for us and our families. We should approach any such judgment with care and compassion. As much as we can, we should judge people's situations rather than

judging the people themselves. Whenever possible, we should refrain from making judgments until we have an adequate knowledge of the facts. And we should always be sensitive to the Holy Spirit, who can guide our decisions."[166]

The three key principles of making good judgments are:

1. As much as we can, we should judge people's situations rather than judge the people themselves.

2. Whenever possible, we should refrain from making judgments until we have an adequate knowledge of the facts.

3. And we should always be sensitive to the Holy Spirit, who can guide our decisions.

As you look at these three principles, decide which of them you are pretty good at. Congrats! Keep it up! Next, identify one that you may struggle with and pray this week for God to help you in that specific way. Did it make a difference?

1 SAMUEL 17—THE "TRANSFORMERS PRINCIPLE" (20 MINUTES)

I grew up watching Saturday morning cartoons in the 1980s. *Transformers* was one of my favorite cartoons to watch. Essentially, the show is about a race of giant super-intelligent robots that can transform into vehicles and other objects. Part of what made *Transformers* so important to me was their theme song. In it, they would sing about how Transformers aren't always what they seem on the outside. This is meant to teach that people and things can have a far deeper hidden power and meaning.

A similar principle is taught in the movie *Shrek*, when the ogre Shrek claims, "Ogres are like onions. . . . Onions have layers. Ogres have layers."

When we look at the story of David and Goliath as *only* an underdog story, we are missing other layers that may be just as hopeful for us. There is more to David than meets the eye. David has layers. Watch the following TED Talk by best-selling author Malcolm Gladwell.[167] I am not sure all of his claims are entirely accurate, but notice how Malcolm's research uncovers deeper layers

165 *The Hebrew Bible, vol. 2*, "Prophets" (2019), 206.

166 Gospel Topics, LDS Gospel Library, "Judging Others."
167 Presented at TEDS Alon, NY. September 2013.

of David and Goliath than we normally consider. Pay special attention to how the Lord had been preparing David throughout his young life "for such a time as this" (Esther 4:14).

(or google "TED Talk Malcolm Gladwell: The Unheard Story of David and Goliath")

Just as David was prepared from a young age to bless the lives of the people in his community, can you identify some experiences you've had in your past that have prepared you for significant challenges?

Let me illustrate with one example. In a seminary class a few years ago, we were talking specifically about preparing for full-time missions and future decisions. After a few minutes of discussion, one student blurted out, "I have always wanted to serve a mission. But how can I testify to strangers of the importance of families being together forever when my parents have been divorced most of my life?"

Based on what you've learned today about being prepared, what are some ways you would answer her question?

JUNE 20–26
"THY KINGDOM SHALL BE ESTABLISHED FOR EVER"
2 SAMUEL 5–7; 11–12; 1 KINGS 3; 8; 11

God's Message to Me from This Section

---

2 SAMUEL 11–12—DRAWING ON YOUR HEAD (10 MINUTES)

Get a piece of paper, pen or pencil, and something hard to write on for everyone (like a book). Or simply use paper plates.

Put the piece of paper on the hard object, and put both on your head (or put a plate on your head). Each person must finish drawing all the steps before they can take the paper (or plate) off their head. Are you ready to have some fun?

1. Draw a tree. When you're done, put your arm down but keep the paper/plate on your head.

2. Draw some nice grass and flowers under the tree. Put your arm down again but keep the paper on your head.

3. Draw a bird's nest in the tree with at least one bird in it. When you're done, you can take the paper off your head.

How did it go? Whose is the best? Whose is the worst? You may want to give small treats to them.

What do trees, grass, flowers, and birds all have in common? (All of them heavily rely on seeds for their survival.)

A common theme in all of scripture is the law of the harvest. You reap what you sow. Can you sow the seeds of an orange tree and reap bananas? No. David is a fascinating study on the law of the harvest. In many ways, he is just like Alma the Younger but in reverse. David began his life by sowing seeds of trust in God and influencing through service. Later in life, he began sowing seeds of selfishness and pride.

As I have been taught principles from the story of Bathsheba, Uriah, and David, it seems to always turn into a lesson about pornography and chastity. My challenge for you is to dig deeper. What other principles can you learn from this tragic story that have nothing to do with pornography and chastity?

Here are a couple of acronyms that have helped me explore other important principles. They aren't great, so please make improvements that will help you.

D	eception
A	gency
V	engence (or pride)
I	nfluence (both + and - influence)
D	isconnection (from relationships with God and other

Here is a simpler one:

D	ecisions
A	re a
V	ery
I	mportant
D	octrine

1 KINGS 3—GIFTS! (10 MINUTES)

Identify two to three gifts, talents, or attributes that have brought you confidence and have helped you have a positive impact on others. If you are studying in a group, please help each other identify these. To help you brainstorm, read the following insights from Elder Marvin J. Ashton:

> Let us review some of these less-conspicuous gifts: the gift of asking; the gift of listening; the gift of hearing and using a still, small voice; the gift of being able to weep; the gift of avoiding contention; the gift of being agreeable; the gift of avoiding vain repetition; the gift of seeking that which is righteous; the gift of not passing judgment; the gift of looking to God for guidance; the gift of being a disciple; the gift of caring for others; the gift of being able to ponder; the gift of offering prayer; the

gift of bearing a mighty testimony; and the gift of receiving the Holy Ghost.[168]

As you look at the gifts, talents, or attributes you identified, what are some personal insecurities your gifts help combat?

Solomon, one of David's sons, became his successor. King Solomon is historically known for his incredible wisdom. The book of Proverbs is mostly a record kept to preserve Solomon's wisdom. But King Solomon did not begin his leadership with confident wisdom; his story began with insecurity. Read 1 Kings 3:3–9 and identify some of Solomon's strengths. Also identify some of his insecurities.

As you read this quote from President George Q. Cannon, think about how Solomon is a great scriptural example of humbly seeking useful gifts: "If any of us are imperfect, it is our duty to pray for the gift that will make us perfect. Have I imperfections? I am full of them. What is my duty? To pray to God to give me the gifts that will correct these imperfections. If I am an angry man, it is my duty to pray for charity, which suffereth long and is kind. . . . So with all the gifts of the Gospel. They are intended for this purpose."[169]

Using the invitation from President Cannon, what is one gift you feel you need that will provide both confidence and a positive impact on others you serve?

As you read the rest of 1 Kings 3, notice the wisdom of Solomon in an impossible situation.

1 KINGS 8—ARE YOU BETTER THAN I? (15 MINUTES)

In the lesson for May 2–8, covering Exodus 35–40 and Leviticus 1; 16; 19, I included a temple quiz. Either go back and take that quiz again or take this quiz.[170] This quiz is much harder! The first time I took it, I scored 11/15. Can you do better than I?

168 "'There Are Many Gifts,'" *Ensign*, November 1987.
169 "Discourse by President George Q. Cannon," Millennial Star, Apr. 23, 1894, 258–261.
170 "Can You Identify These 15 Latter-day Saint Temples . . . From the Sky?," posted June 14, 2019, https://thirdhour.org/blog/quiz/hard/quiz-temples-sky/.

King Solomon was authorized by the Lord to build a temple. 1 Kings 5–8 is the detailed process and purpose for building this temple. Solomon's temple was unique in scripture because it was so ornate and beautiful. Solomon's temple genuinely reflected the best mortals could give to build a house of the Lord. I would encourage you to focus primarily on 1 Kings 8:22–54. It is the dedicatory prayer Solomon offered as he "stood before the altar of the Lord in the presence of all the congregation of Israel, and spread forth his hands toward heaven."[171] In what ways does Solomon's prayer help us focus on the purpose of temple worship? Here are a few of my favorites:

- 1 Kings 8:23—The temple is a house of walking with God in covenant relationships.

- 1 Kings 8:29—The Lord puts His name on those who seek Him in temples.

- 1 Kings 8:34, 36, 39—The temple is a house of forgiveness.

- 1 Kings 8:45—The temple is a house of prayer.

- 1 Kings 8:47–48—The temple is a house of atonement.

1 KINGS 6–7—NEPHI'S TEMPLE, SOLOMON'S TEMPLE—A LESSON ABOUT COMPARISON (5 MINUTES)

The incredible detail and expense of Solomon's temple is described in 1 Kings 6–7. After Nephi separated from Laman and Lemuel in the promised land, he and his people eventually built a temple. Nephi compared his temple to Solomon's: "And I, Nephi, did build a temple; and I did construct it after the manner of the temple of Solomon save it were not built of so many precious things; for they were not to be found upon the land, wherefore, it could not be built like unto Solomon's temple." No matter what Nephi and his people tried, their temple would never compare to Solomon's. This feeling of comparison plagues many of us today. No

matter how hard we try, we never feel like we measure up to the ideal.

Nephi concluded this verse with a powerful principle that can help us when we are overwhelmed by comparisons: "But the manner of the construction was like unto the temple of Solomon; and the workmanship thereof was exceedingly fine."[172]

Nephi understood that their *offering* was more important than the overall *outcome*. Nephi did not anticipate that they would build an exact replica of Solomon's temple, because he knew he wasn't expected to. Instead, they built their temple "like unto the temple of Solomon." Concluding with the testimony, "And the workmanship thereof was exceedingly fine."

As you go throughout this week, recognize areas where comparison is not healthy for you. Think about what Nephi taught, and see if it makes a difference.

---

171 Verse 22.

172 2 Nephi 5:16.

JUNE 27–JULY 3
"IF THE LORD BE GOD, FOLLOW HIM"
1 KINGS 17–19

God's Message to Me from This Section

OVERVIEW OF 1–2 KINGS—LET'S GET COMPLICATED (10 MINUTES)

The books of 1–2 Kings are imperative to understand in the narrative of the Old Testament moving forward. It's about to get much more complicated. The following video will really help you understand how 1–2 Kings sets up the rest of the history of the Old Testament.[173] I will put this same video in the lesson two weeks from now to review again. My hope is that the repetition will bring clarity to your study of the second half of the Old Testament.

(or google "BibleProject Overview: 1–2 Kings")

1 KINGS 17:7–22—FAITH IN PROPHETIC PROMISES BRINGS LIFE (15 MINUTES)

Here are some recent promises President Russell M. Nelson has given in general conference. As you read through them, *underline* what the Lord is asking us to do and *circle* the life-giving words in each promise.

- "I promise that as you increase your capacity to receive revelation, the Lord will bless you with increased direction for your life and with boundless gifts of the Spirit."[174]

- "I am not saying that the days ahead will be easy, but I promise you that the future will be glorious for those who are prepared and who continue to prepare to be instruments in the Lord's hands."[175]

- "I promise that as we create places of security, prepare our minds to be faithful to God, and never stop preparing, God will bless us. He will 'deliver us; yea, insomuch that he [will] speak peace to our souls, and [will] grant unto us great faith, and . . . cause us that we [can] hope for our deliverance in him.'"[176]

- "I bless you with an increased desire and ability to obey the laws of God. I promise that as you do, you will be showered with blessings, including greater courage, increased personal revelation, sweeter harmony in your homes, and joy even amid uncertainty."[177]

- "Previously, I promised that if we will 'do our best to restore the correct name of the Lord's Church,' He

---

173 BibleProject, 1 & 2 Kings Old Testament Overviews, https://bibleproject.com/explore/video/kings/.

174 "Embrace the Future with Faith," *Ensign*, November 2020, 75–76.

175 Ibid.

176 Ibid.

177 A New Normal," *Ensign*, Nov. 2020, 119.

will 'pour down His power and blessings upon the heads of the Latter-day Saints, the likes of which we have never seen.' I renew that promise today."[178]

- "I promise that as you increase your time in temple and family history work, you will increase and improve your ability to hear Him."[179]

- "What will happen as you more intentionally hear, hearken, and heed what the Savior has said and what He is saying now through His prophets? I promise that you will be blessed with additional power to deal with temptation, struggles, and weakness. I promise miracles in your marriage, family relationships, and daily work. And I promise that your capacity to feel joy will increase even if turbulence increases in your life."[180]

Can you think of any other recent promises President Nelson has made? How has following a prophet brought life and light to you? What blessing are you still waiting to be fulfilled?

The widow of Zarephath is a tremendous example of trusting in prophetic promises. Her story is literally about life and death for her and her son. But her trust in God brought life to her family of two. She is also an example of Christ: "Greater love hath no [woman] than this, that a [Mom] lay down [her] life for [her child]" (John 15:13). She did all that was in her power to survive, trusting that God would bring her a feast during a time of famine. Open to 1 Kings 17:7–22 and follow along as you watch the following video.

(or google "Gospel Media Library, Widow of Zarephath")

4 PRINCIPLES LEARNED FROM THE WIDOW OF ZAREPHATH

1. Be as honest about your situation as you need to be, but don't give up.

2. God will send someone to help you.

3. Try to replace fear of outcome with trust in God.

4. Just because we go through difficult seasons in our lives, it does not mean God is against us. We can still have a feast of heavenly blessings during mortal famines.

1 KINGS 19:11–13—"HEAR HIM" SCRIPTURES AND STORIES (10 MINUTES)

Run around your home and grab anything you see that helps you feel safe. So many things work. You have three minutes. GO!

If you are studying as a group, have each person share a few things they found. Specifically share the unsafe scenario in which this item provides a feeling of safety. (For example, I could grab my toothbrush. I always know I can have good breath because of my toothbrush. A feeling of fresh breath is safe for me.)

President Russell M. Nelson taught, "Our Father knows that when we are surrounded by uncertainty and fear, what will help us the very most is to hear His Son." President Nelson then made this important contrast, "The adversary is clever. For millennia he has been making good look evil and evil look good. His messages tend to be loud, bold, and boastful. However, messages from our Heavenly Father are strikingly different. He communicates simply, quietly, and with such stunning plainness that we cannot misunderstand Him."[181]

Read 1 Kings 19:11–13 and notice how the voice of the Lord spoke to Elijah. Take a few minutes and see if you can find scriptures or scripture stories that teach principles of how to better identify the Lord's voice in our lives. Here are a few of my favorites if you need some help:

- Helaman 5:30, 45–47

- 1 Nephi 18:1–3

- Alma 5:38, 41

- 1 Samuel 3:4–10

- Doctrine and Covenants 42:61

- Doctrine and Covenants 45:56–57

Do you have any personal stories you can share in which God has spoken to you?

---

178 "Opening the Heavens for Help," *Ensign*, May 2020, 73.
179 "Hear Him," *Ensign*, May 2020, 90.
180 Ibid.

181 "Hear Him," *Ensign*, May 2020, 89.

JULY 4–10
"THERE IS A PROPHET IN ISRAEL"
2 KINGS 2–7

God's Message to Me from This Section

FINDING THE MISSION OF CHRIST IN THE LIVES OF HIS PROPHETS (10 MINUTES)

From Abraham, Isaac, and Moses to Joseph of Egypt and Elijah,[182] elements of the mission of Jesus Christ are found in the lives of His prophets.

---

182 Adapted from Kerry Muhlestein, *The Essential Old Testament Companion* (Covenant Communications [2013]), 275.

Elijah's life was sought by royalty (1 Kings 19:2; 2 Kings 1)	Christ's life was sought by Herod (see Matthew 2)
Elijah miraculously multiplied food for the widow from Zarephath (see 1 Kings 17:13–16)	Christ multiplied food for the multitude (see Matthew 14:17; 15:34; Mark 6:38; 8:7; John 6:9)
Elijah raised the widow's son from the dead (see 1 Kings 17:17–23)	Christ raised a widow's son, Jairus's daughter, and Lazarus from the dead (see Luke 7:12–15; Matthew 9:18–25; John 11)
Elijah controlled storms and rain (1 Kings 17:1; 18:38, 44–45; 2 Kings 1:10–14)	Christ controlled storms and wind (see Matthew 8:23–27; Mark 4:35–41; Luke 8:23–34)
Elijah demonstrated power over false prophets (1 Kings 18)	Christ demonstrated power over false spirits (see Mark 1:23–26; 3:11; 5:8; 9:25)
Elijah sought refuge in Sinai at an angel's behest (1 Kings 18:5–8)	Christ sought refuge in Egypt at an angel's behest (see Matthew 2:13–14)
Elijah was taken up into heaven (2 Kings 2:11)	Christ was taken up into heaven (see Acts 1:9–11)
Elijah was to come (to the temple) again before the great and dreadful day (see Malachi 4:5–6)	Christ will come to the temple suddenly before the great and dreadful day (see Malachi 3:1–2)

Do you remember the paper-airplane activity you did a few weeks ago as we studied Ruth and 1 Samuel 1–3? The purpose was to identify a few statements or questions to focus your study on what's most important to you. Please go back and reread your purpose statements.

Now choose one of the scripture references about the Savior's life in the right column of the previous chart. The goal is to see if you can connect one of your purpose statements to an example from the life of Jesus.

For example, if one of the statements I identified from the airplane activity was to *find connection points to Jesus Christ,* and then I choose to study how Christ controlled storms and wind,[183] I learn that winds and waves are an important part of life because they direct my desires to the calming, peaceful power of Jesus Christ. Knowing He can bring a sense of calmness and peace into life during my overwhelming experiences strengthens my testimony in His divinity. Jesus Christ is worth trusting.

Your turn!

2 KINGS 5:1–15—NAAMAN AND THE TEMPLE (10 MINUTES)

2 Kings 5 is incredible because it teaches the entire plan of redemption in one chapter. As mentioned in this book a few times already, the plan of redemption is the core teaching of the temple.[184] Elder David A. Bednar explained that a key purpose of home-centered and Church-supported learning is to focus on temple preparation in the home. He taught, "Indeed, temple preparation is most effective in our homes. But many Church members are unsure about what appropriately can and cannot be said regarding the temple experience outside of the temple."[185] My purpose with Naaman is to help you see the covenant pattern in Naaman's life. This is especially interesting because Naaman is the captain of the host in Syria, not Israel.

- Naaman was seeking deliverance from leprosy.

- Naaman experienced trials of faith and ego.

- Naaman received further light and knowledge through the testimony of friends and directions from a prophet.

- Through obedience and sacrifice, Naaman was washed clean, renewed, and reborn.

- Through personal experience, Naaman knew that healing and deliverance come only through the grace of Jesus Christ.

2 KINGS 5:10–13—NAAMAN AND EXPECTATIONS (10 MINUTES)

Watch the following video and see what similarities you can find between the video and the story of Naaman. Pay special attention to the role of expectations.

Gospel Library App -> Videos and Images -> Inspirational Messages -> Flecks of Gold

(or google "Flecks of Gold")

Elder Dieter F. Uchtdorf taught,

> First, you need to choose to incline your heart to God. Strive each day to find Him. Learn to love Him. And then let that love inspire you to learn, understand, and follow His teachings and learn to keep God's commandments. The restored gospel of Jesus Christ is given to us in a plain and simple way that a child can understand. Yet the gospel of Jesus Christ has the answers to the most complex questions in life and has such profound depth and complexity that even with a lifetime of study and pondering, we can scarcely comprehend even the smallest part.
>
> If you hesitate in this adventure because you doubt your ability, remember that discipleship is not about doing things

---

183 Mark 4:35–41.

184 See May 2–8: Exodus 35–40; Leviticus 1; 16; 19; and May 20–June 5, Judges 2–4; 6–8; 13–16.

185 "Prepared to Obtain Every Needful Thing," *Ensign,* May 2019, 103.

perfectly; it's about doing things intentionally. It is your choices that show what you truly are, far more than your abilities.[186]

In what ways does Elder Uchtdorf help us shift expectations and focus on the small and simple things we can do every day?

What are some small and simple things you do consistently that have made a big difference?

What small and simple things could you do on Saturdays to bring more peace to your Sundays?

In what ways is *Come, Follow Me* like the story of Naaman? How can Elder Uchtdorf's words help manage your expectations when you aren't doing *Come, Follow Me* perfectly?

2 KINGS 6:1–17—"AND THE LORD OPENED THE EYES OF THE YOUNG MAN; AND HE SAW" (10 MINUTES)

President Thomas S. Monson taught, "Our Heavenly Father is aware of our needs and will help us as we call upon Him for assistance. I believe that no concern of ours is too small or insignificant. The Lord is in the details of our lives."[187]

The Lord was not only interested in the vision of the prophet Elisha, but He was also interested in the vision of a young man who served Elisha. Read 2 Kings 6:1–17 and notice how the Lord and His prophet helped another to see. You may notice

- the young man was really afraid.

- he reached out for help, honestly expressing his feelings.

- prayer was offered, and the Lord used another to help the young man see.

- faith and trust in the Lord was increased. The young man knew the Lord cared about him.

Now watch the following video and look for consistencies between this young woman's experience and the young man's. After the video, discuss what you hope to remember from this story in 2 Kings 6.

Gospel Library -> Audiences -> Youth -> Youth Media -> Youth Videos -> Heavenly Father Knows Me

(or google "Heavenly Father Knows Me")

What experiences did you have when you were young that helped you see that Heavenly Father really does care about you?

---

186 "Your Great Adventure," *Ensign*, November 2019, 87.
187 "Consider the Blessings," *Ensign*, November 2012, 88.

JULY 11–17
"HE TRUSTED IN THE LORD GOD OF ISRAEL"
2 KINGS 17–25

God's Message to Me from This Section

LET'S REVIEW (15 MINUTES)

Many books in the Old Testament were written during the historical timeline described in 1–2 Kings. Anything written after the death of Samuel and before Babylonian captivity fits this timeline. These books include Ecclesiastes, Amos, Jonah, Hosea, Micah, Isaiah, Ezekiel, and Jeremiah.

Watch the following video from two weeks ago.[188] What do you understand about the Old Testament now that you didn't know before you started studying 1–2 Kings?

2 KINGS 19, 22–23—LIGHTHOUSES (15 MINUTES)

Please begin by drawing a simple lighthouse on a piece of paper. You could include ocean waves, a mountainside and any other details you wish as you read.

There are so many stories of nations, families, and individuals who become lost. Experiencing the difficult feeling of being lost is clearly an important part of our mortal experience, or it would not be so universal. It's interesting to me that God doesn't seem to worry much about describing to us how Lehi accumulated his wealth; the Book of Mormon begins when he loses it. Luke, in the New Testament, is a person deeply focused on loss. In fact, Luke 15 is a chapter dedicated to experiences of loss. Luke covers Jesus's parables of the lost coin, the lost sheep, and the prodigal son.

In 2 Kings 17–25, covenant Israel is dealing with devastating loss. Many lose their land of inheritance, their freedom, and their lives to the Assyrians. We even call these people the *lost* ten tribes. Another scriptural word for *lost* is *scattered*. One of the greatest losses they endure, however, is the loss of their identity.

What are some of the ways you have felt like you are losing your identity as a child of Heavenly Parents who is worth saving?

One of the main ways the Lord helps *find* us, or *gather* us, is through others. Two key figures you will study this week are King Hezekiah and King Josiah. We are

---

188 BibleProject, 1 & 2 Kings Old Testament Overviews, (https://bibleproject.com/explore/video/kings/).

also introduced to a prophet named Isaiah.[189] As you read 2 Kings 19, 22–23, look for ways Hezekiah and Josiah helped gather others in.

Watch the following video describing not only the importance of a lighthouse in a storm, but also the lower lights. King Hezekiah, King Josiah, and Isaiah are all lower lights burning brightly, with their flames of testimony desperately trying to help those who are searching to be gathered into the safety of Christ's arms.

(or google "Keep the Lower Lights Burning—The Spoken Word")

Go back to your lighthouse drawing and include a lower light below the lighthouse to help guide ships to safety in the darkness. While doing this, consider the following questions:

- Is there a character or two in the Old Testament who has been a lower light guiding you closer to the Savior this year?

- Who in your home is a lower light to you?

- In what ways have latter-day prophets been a lower light in leading you closer to Christ?

- Will you pray to be a lower light in the life of someone this week? Or maybe you desperately need a lower light in your life. Will you pray to find someone who can be this lower light for you?

You may want to take the time to sing and analyze the words of hymn 335, "Brightly Beams Our Father's Mercy."

INTRODUCING . . . HULDAH! (5 MINUTES)

Because many of the next books in the Old Testament refer back to this time period in 2 Kings, I am going to go in a different direction to include a brief profile on one the most captivating women in scripture. Let me introduce you to Huldah by highlighting what we know

of her and her impact in Jerusalem during a critical time. (For all verses in the Old Testament referring to Huldah, see 2 Kings 22:12–20; 2 Chronicles 34:22–28.)

- Huldah was one of only a few prophetesses mentioned in the Bible (Miriam, Deborah, and Hannah).

- Jeremiah and Huldah were related. While Jeremiah was preaching repentance primarily to the men in Jerusalem, Huldah was doing the same to the women.

- It is interesting to note that King Josiah sent five servants to Huldah, not Jeremiah, for guidance. While there are a variety of possible explanations for this, it's important to note that Huldah was considered an equal to Jeremiah in spiritual credibility and authority.

- Huldah used the holy prophetic utterance, "Thus saith the Lord" four times (2 Chronicles 34:23–24, 26–27) as she interpreted scripture for King Josiah.

- Huldah was also well known for her intelligence and capacity to educate the people.

- Huldah's influence was primarily felt during King Josiah's reign, specifically around 622 BC.

- Because Lehi and Sariah in the Book of Mormon were subjects to Josiah during the same time, they might have known Huldah and her husband. It is also possible that they lived in the same area of Jerusalem!

- During the mortal life of Jesus, there were sets of gates that led worshippers to the Temple Mount. The Mishnah refers to the gates collectively as the Huldah Gates.

---

189 See 2 Kings 19:5.

JULY 18–24
"I AM DOING A GREAT WORK"
EZRA 1; 3–7; NEHEMIAH 2; 4–6; 8

God's Message to Me from This Section

THE TEMPLE IS BACK! EZRA 1:3–7 (15 MINUTES)

After only a generation, the Persians conquered the Babylonian empire. Cyrus, King of Persia, allowed the exiled Jews in Babylon to return to Jerusalem. Although Jerusalem would be under Persian rule, Cyrus allowed them to rebuild the temple. The books of Ezra and Nehemiah specifically focus on rebuilding testimonies as the people rebuild their beloved temple.

This also becomes a turning point for the Jewish nation. Before Babylonian exile, they struggled for hundreds of years with idolatry. The returning Jews clearly knew their painful exile was a result of their idolatry, and as they returned, they were determined to put away their idol worship and instead worship the Lord. However, turning from the idol worship of the past led to another major struggle as they moved toward the birth of Jesus Christ. For many, the law itself became their worship rather than the Giver of the law. Before, they did not adhere strictly enough to the law, but moving forward, they held on to the law too tightly, eventually squeezing out the spirit and leaving many only with the letter.

Draw a large but simple picture of the temple nearest you (or use the following as an outline).

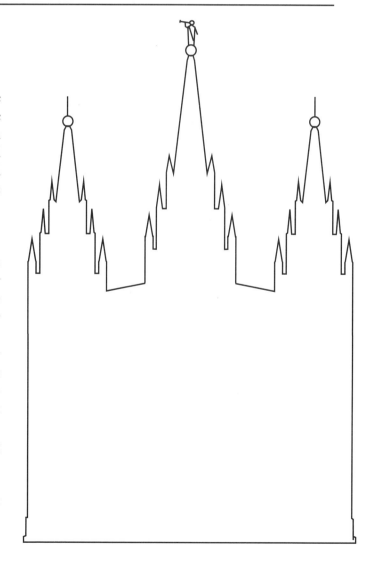

Inside of the temple, write the words that come to mind that represent its purpose and your feelings. Leave room because you will add to this. If you study in a group, give each person three to five minutes to do this before moving on.

As you read the book of Ezra, notice the spiritual rebuilding the Lord is doing with His people. As you read the following examples, please add words inside your temple that impress you from these verses.

- Ezra 1:1–6—The Spirit of the Lord helped gather many to participate in the rebuild.

- Ezra 2:64–69—Thousands "offered freely for the house of God. . . . They gave of their ability."

- Ezra 3:11—Rather than blaming God for their past heartaches, they praised Him for His goodness and mercy.

- Ezra 3:12–13—Their shouts of joy were "heard afar off."

- Ezra 5:2—Influential leaders gratefully participated in the rebuild, including Zerubbabel and "the prophets of God helping them."

- Ezra 6:16–22—The house was dedicated! But more importantly, so were the people.

- Ezra 7:10—Ezra's heart was prepared "to seek the law of the Lord, and to do it, and to teach in Israel."[190]

- Ezra 7:15–17, 27–28—The people learned to draw strength from the Lord through offering freely unto Him.

When you are finished, give each person the opportunity to share at least one word that is important to them and why.

NEHEMIAH 2:13; 3:13–14—THE "DUNG GATE PRINCIPLE" (10 MINUTES)

When thinking about their rebuilding the walls and gates of Jerusalem, I picture towering walls and impressive gates—walls that protect from enemies, walls that testify of peace and safety to Jerusalem's residences. I imagine well-protected, strategically placed, and culturally significant gates. Wouldn't it be wonderful to

be assigned to guard the gates of Jerusalem? I used to think that until I learned about the dung gate.

Because of the many animal sacrifices in the temple, there was a lot of . . . dung. Therefore, the dung gate was primarily used to discard animal dung. Certain temple workers were specifically assigned to remove dung from the temple grounds using this gate. How would you feel if this were your stewardship assignment? Can you already smell the relevance of the dung gate?

Although dung-gate assignments are not awesome, dung itself is often repurposed to bring life. In Jacob 5, the Lord of the vineyard used dung to fertilize tender trees so they could bring forth much fruit. What are some ways the Lord could bring life through some of your dung-gate assignments?

In studying Doctrine and Covenants and Church history last year, we learned of a time when Church historian Oliver Cowdery was called on a mission. Oliver was a prolific and gifted writer and a fantastic historian during the very early days of the Church, but his mission call would leave a major vacancy. Who would serve as the Church historian while Oliver was gone? Joseph felt inspired to call David Whitmer. David responded, "I would rather not do it."[191] David may have considered this calling a dung-gate assignment, but think of how important the recorded history of the Church is to us today. Can you think of callings, assignments, and stewardships in the Church that *you* would personally refer to as working at the dung gate?

One other aspect of the dung-gate principle is taught in Nehemiah 6:4. As Nehemiah managed the temple rebuild, his enemies continually tried to distract him. His response reflects his vision and commitment to what they were trying to accomplish: "I am doing a great work, so that I cannot come down."

Let me conclude the dung-gate principle with a story that's rooted in history but leans more toward a parable. You can find variations of this story online. Whether we are managing a large-scale temple rebuild or cleaning the church bathrooms on a Saturday morning, we are still contributing to "a great work."

---

190 The sons of Mosiah were similarly prepared (see Alma 17:2–3, 9–11).

---

191 See the section heading to Doctrine and Covenants 47.

The St. Paul Cathedral in London was significantly burned during the Great Fire of London in 1666. The world-famous architect Christopher Wren was commissioned to rebuild the structure.

Five years into the project, Wren noticed three bricklayers working on the cathedral. One bricklayer was crouched down, one was half standing, and the third was standing tall and working much harder than the others. "What are you doing?" Wren asked the first bricklayer. "I'm stacking bricks." Wren asked the second bricklayer the same question. That bricklayer responded, "I am building a wall." Wren approached the third and asked, "What are you doing?" This hardworking bricklayer exclaimed, "I am building a cathedral to the Almighty!"

NEHEMIAH 8:4–8—A PROPHET NAMED EZRA (10 MINUTES)

Before this week, did you even know there was a book of Nehemiah in the scriptures? So, is the book of Nehemiah really that relevant to us as members of The Church of Jesus Christ of Latter-day Saints? The fact that I'm even asking you this question is probably your answer. Nehemiah 8 has two very *Latter-day Saint* themes. In fact, your familiarity with the Book of Mormon, temple, and modern prophets will open your eyes to Nehemiah 8.

In Nehemiah 8:4–8, we read about a prophet named Ezra, who stood at "a pulpit of wood" and "opened the book in the sight of all the people." Ezra's purpose was to recommit them to reading the word of God. The people responded with an attitude of humility and recommitment to feast upon the word of God with gratitude and enthusiasm.

In October 1986, the exact same thing happened! A prophet named Ezra stood at a pulpit made of wood in the tabernacle and opened the Book of Mormon to the eyes of the Saints to expand its meaning. President Ezra Taft Benson's purpose was to recommit the people to reading the word of God with gratitude and enthusiasm.

President Benson began his talk by speaking of the gift of the Book of Mormon. He taught,

> My beloved brethren and sisters, today I would like to speak about one of the most significant gifts given to the world in modern times. The gift I am thinking of is more important than any of the inventions that have come out of the industrial and technological revolutions. This is a gift of greater value to mankind than even the many wonderful advances we have seen in modern medicine. It is of greater worth to mankind than the development of flight or space travel. I speak of the gift of the Book of Mormon, given to mankind 156 years ago.[192]

Among so many other beautiful teachings, President Benson shared Joseph Smith's testimony of the Book of Mormon found in the Introduction of the Book of Mormon: "I told the brethren that the Book of Mormon was the most correct of any book on earth, and the keystone of our religion, and a man would get nearer to God by abiding by its precepts, than by any other book."

Take a few minutes to rekindle your testimony of the Book of Mormon. How has this book been a gift to you? In what ways have you drawn closer to Christ through the Book of Mormon? What Book of Mormon verses or stories are you most grateful for?

NEHEMIAH 8:14–18—FORTS AND FEASTS (15 MINUTES)

Two of the most important feasts in ancient Israel were the Passover feast and the Feast of Tabernacles (or *Sukkot* in Hebrew). They held the feast of the Passover each year in the spring primarily to commemorate the new life Jehovah gave the children of Israel when He liberated them from Egypt. In Christ's time, this feast took on a new meaning in addition to its original meaning. The last week of Jesus Christ's life took place during Passover week, thus redefining the week by adding the promise that all of God's creations will receive eternal life through Christ.

---

192 "The Book of Mormon—Keystone of Our Religion," *Ensign*, November 1986, 4–7.

Like Passover, the Feast of Tabernacles was a yearly celebration held in the fall after the harvest was gathered in. This feast included a festival of lights. It was during this week that Jesus Christ declared, "I am the light of the world: he that followeth me shall not walk in darkness, but shall have the light of life" (John 8:12).

These two feasts are deeply integrated into our latter-day culture even if we don't fully recognize their influence. Joseph Smith had his vision in the spring of 1820. The Church was organized on April 6, 1830. We hold general conferences in the spring and fall each year. Jesus Christ appeared in the Kirtland temple on April 3, 1836. In fact, this was the same week Jews around the world celebrated Passover!

In Nehemiah 8:14–18, we read about the Jewish people building "booths" for their families to commemorate the Feast of Tabernacles. To understand this significance, please watch the following video from Book of Mormon Central that connects Nehemiah 8, Mosiah 2, and our modern general conferences.[193]

(or google "Why Did the Nephites Stay in Their Tents During King Benjamin's Speech?")

If that isn't fascinating enough, watch this next short video showing why Moroni delivered the gold plates to Joseph Smith on the date he did.[194]

(or google "Why Did Moroni Deliver the Plates on September 22?")

Look back on your study of Ezra and Nehemiah this week. What is one personal highlight that you want to remember, and why?

---

193 "Why Did the Nephites Stay in Their Tents During King Benjamin's Speech?" bookofmormoncentral.org, posted April 18, 2016.
194 "Why Did Moroni Deliver the Plates on September 22?" bookofmormoncentral.org, posted September 22, 2016.

JULY 25–31

"THOU ART COME . . . FOR SUCH A TIME AS THIS"

ESTHER

God's Message to Me from This Section

WHEN OR WHERE WOULD I LIVE? (20 MINUTES)

If you could have lived during any other time in history, when would it have been and why? If you could have been born in any other place in the present, where would it have been and why? After contemplating and discussing these questions, consider this one:

Why has the Lord sent me to the earth at this time and placed me in my circumstances?

While Ezra and others were rebuilding the temple in Jerusalem, Esther was a Jewish orphan who lived approximately one thousand miles away in the prominent Persian city of Susa, or Shushan. Around the time of Esther, the vast Persian empire had a population of 50 million people. The estimated population of the world at that time was 100–160 million, meaning Persians accounted for roughly thirty to fifty percent of all people on the earth! There is no reason we should know about Esther—one person in that massive sea of people. So why do we? I'm sure there are many possible answers to this question. To me, the story of Esther is a heaven-sent testimony that in the vastness of mortality, in the loneliness of obscurity, our Parents in Heaven know us personally and have a divine work for each of us. We matter to Them! In a general conference talk titled "You Matter to Him," Elder Dieter F. Uchtdorf testified:

This is a paradox of man: compared to God, man is nothing; yet we are everything to God. While against the backdrop of infinite creation we may appear to be nothing, we have a spark of eternal fire burning within our breast. We have the incomprehensible promise of exaltation—worlds without end—within our grasp. And it is God's great desire to help us reach it.[195]

As you read this week, I invite you to imagine you are studying with Esther. Included are a few questions I've struggled with that Esther is uniquely equipped to answer. You can use these or others you come up with, but the point is to write down some of the ways you think Esther would answer these questions for you.

Question: Do I really matter?

Possible scriptural answers:

---

195 "You Matter to Him," *Ensign*, November 2011, 20.

Esther's response:

Question: Is there any purpose for me? If so, how do I find it?

Possible scriptural answers:

Esther's response:

Question: Do I have anything of value to offer others?

Possible scriptural answers:

Esther's response:

Question: How can I have courage when I am really afraid?

Possible scriptural answers:

Esther's response:

Question: What can I do to see the hand of God more in my life?

Possible scriptural answers:

WE WORSHIP A GOD WHO PATIENTLY NOURISHES (10 MINUTES)

The book of Esther is also unique because it never mentions God specifically by name. But while His name is not anywhere in the text, His influence is everywhere!

There is a beautiful connecting truth taught in the allegory of the olive tree in Jacob 5:21–23 in the Book of Mormon. In this small interaction, the Lord of the vineyard and a servant went to what they described as the "poorest spot in all the land of the vineyard." In verse 22, they observed that this poor spot had "brought forth much fruit." What a miracle! In verse 23, they continued to a "spot of ground [that] was poorer than the first," and they also found that after nourishing it "this long time," it "hath brought forth much fruit."

Who do you know who has had a tough life? Like Esther, it seems like they were planted in a poor spot of the vineyard. Does this describe you at all?

As you watch the following video, notice the small but significant ways the Lord nourished Aaron. Like Esther, Aaron found divine strength, value, and purpose in his life as he relied on the power of God.

Gospel Library app -> Youth -> Youth Media -> Youth Videos -> Wheelz: Overcoming Is Possible

(or google "Wheelz: Overcoming Is Possible")

AUGUST 1–7
"YET WILL I TRUST IN HIM"
JOB 1–3; 12–14; 19; 21–24; 38–40; 42

God's Message to Me from This Section

PARENT ADVICE (10 MINUTES)

Can you remember advice from parents, teachers, or others? Some of it is ridiculous, some of it is life-changing, and some of it is both.

President Henry B. Eyring has shared, "My mother used to say to me when I complained that things were hard, 'If you are on the right path, it will always be uphill.'"[196] This is a good way to start the book of Job. Another good way to start the book of Job is to read the very first verse in the very first chapter: "There was a man in the land of Uz, whose name was Job; and that man was perfect and upright, and one that feared God, and eschewed [or turned away from] evil."

Before we go any further, let me address a few things. We do not know *who* wrote the book of Job, and we do not know *when* it was written. However, we do know the book was written as a literary play, which leads many of us to wonder if Job was a real person or simply a character written into an ancient drama. Maybe he was both. Maybe there was an ancient play written about a real person. Taking ancient poetic writing and attempting to interpret it as literal happenings is like trying to hammer in a nail using your cell phone—it was never meant for that purpose and is ultimately more harmful than helpful.

Regardless, there are principles and doctrines taught in this book that are very useful for us as we navigate the complexities of mortality. "The book of Job teaches that if a person has a correct knowledge of God and is living a life that is acceptable to God, he will be better able to endure the trials that come upon him."[197]

A CORRECT KNOWLEDGE OF GOD (20 MINUTES)

In the *Lectures on Faith* we learn, "Correct ideas of the character of God are necessary in order to exercise faith in him unto life and salvation; and that without correct ideas of his character, men could not have power to exercise faith in him unto life and salvation, but that correct ideas of his character, as far as his character is concerned in the exercise of faith in him, lay a sure foundation for the exercise of it."

Nephi is a good example of someone who relied on his testimony and knowledge of the character of God to carry him through an important time when he was confused. In vision, Nephi was asked, "Knowest thou the condescension of God?" He replied, "*I know that he loveth his children;* nevertheless, I do not know the

---

196 "Raise the Bar," Brigham Young University–Idaho Devotional, January 25, 2005.

197 Gospel Library, Guide to the Scriptures, "Job."

meaning of all things."[198] When faced with uncertainty, Nephi first trusted in God's loving character to carry him through his lack of understanding.

Look at these scriptures to identify how Job feels about the character of God. You will also notice how his understanding of God positively influences his perspective even though he is simultaneously "full of confusion" (see Job 10:15).

- Job 1:21
- Job 13:13, 15
- Job 19:25–27
- Job 27:2–6
- Job 28:12–13, 28
- Job 42:12

Watch the following video and notice as many consistencies as you can with the book of Job. For example, in Job 13:13, 15, he testified, "Come on me what will. . . . Yet will I trust in him." Through her accident and subsequent recovery, Stephanie better understood what it meant to trust in God and submit to His will. She trusted that her suffering had purpose and was worth the struggle. Her perspective and gratitude for God's plan are beautiful, divine, and deeply motivating. I feel a similar spirit as I read the words of Job.

(or google "Inspirational messages: My New Life LDS video")

To finish, what are some attributes of Jesus Christ you rely on to carry you through suffering, uncertainty, and confusion?

WHY DO THE RIGHTEOUS CHOOSE TO STAY RIGHTEOUS? (15 MINUTES)

A few years ago, I had a seminary student who suffered

an extreme tragedy. During a date a few months into her senior year, she and three friends were in a major car accident. As a result, her date, who was one of her best friends, passed away. The trauma of that experience hung over her and the school like a thick cloud of darkness. Although she was a naturally cheerful and positive person, she found herself in a deep fog of hopelessness and despair. Over the next few months, she constantly felt at war with her own emotions and spirituality. Like Job, she was "full of confusion" (Job 10:15). In my seminary class, she was very open at times about the pain of her experience and that of her friends. In fact, I set aside an entire box of tissues just for her because when she would talk in class, there were almost always tears, which reflected her broken heart.

A few months later, we were talking in class about what peace is and what peace isn't. Near the end, she raised her hand and said something I will never forget. Full of wisdom, faith, and perspective, she taught, "Over the last six months, I have learned that Jesus doesn't necessarily remove the pain. Instead, He blesses us with peace to outweigh the pain. I've learned that the pain is important because it is the path to peace. Pain teaches us why we need peace. I don't think you get to peace without walking through pain." What a discovery!

In the Book of Mormon, Jacob taught, "The things of the wise and the prudent shall be hid from them forever—yea, that happiness which is prepared for the saints" (2 Nephi 9:43). In other words, as we experience trial, tragedy, and trauma, the Lord will help us discover happiness if we continue to trust in Him. However, if we shut the Lord out of our pain, the "happiness which is prepared for the saints" will be hidden from us forever.

So why do the righteous choose to stay righteous? At least one answer is that they have discovered peace in the pain and happiness in heartache. The Apostle Paul called this discovery the "peace of God, which passeth all understanding," which "shall keep [or protect] your hearts and minds through Christ Jesus" (Philippians 4:7).

Like Job and my former student, the following story is another example of discovering "the peace of God, which passeth all understanding." Notice the happiness that was hidden from the teacher who did not share the

198 1 Nephi 11:16–17; emphasis added. Enos and the Brother of Jared are additional examples of relying on the attributes of God when faced with uncertainty (see Enos 1:6; Ether 3:11–12).

same painful pioneer experiences as the old man.

Some years ago President David O. McKay (1873–1970) told of the experience of some of those in the Martin handcart company. Many of these early converts had emigrated from Europe and were too poor to buy oxen or horses and a wagon. They were forced by their poverty to pull handcarts containing all of their belongings across the plains by their own brute strength. President McKay related an occurrence which took place some years after the heroic exodus:

"A teacher, conducting a class, said it was unwise ever to attempt, even to permit them [the Martin handcart company] to come across the plains under such conditions."

Then President McKay quoted an observer who was present in that class: "Some sharp criticism of the Church and its leaders was being indulged in for permitting any company of converts to venture across the plains with no more supplies or protection than a handcart caravan afforded.

"An old man in the corner . . . sat silent and listened as long as he could stand it, then he arose and said things that no person who heard him will ever forget. His face was white with emotion, yet he spoke calmly, deliberately, but with great earnestness and sincerity.

"In substance [he] said, 'I ask you to stop this criticism. You are discussing a matter you know nothing about. Cold historic facts mean nothing here, for they give no proper interpretation of the questions involved. Mistake to send the Handcart Company out so late in the season? Yes. But I was in that company and my wife was in it . . . too. We suffered beyond anything you can imagine and many died of exposure and starvation, but did you ever hear a survivor of that company utter a word of criticism? . . .

"'I have pulled my handcart when I was so weak and weary from illness and lack of food that I could hardly put one foot ahead of the other. I have looked ahead and seen a patch of sand or a hill slope and I have said, I can go only that far and there I must give up, for I cannot pull the load through it.'"

He continues: "'I have gone on to that sand and when I reached it, the cart began pushing me. I have looked back many times to see who was pushing my cart, but my eyes saw no one. I knew then that the angels of God were there.

"'Was I sorry that I chose to come by handcart? No. Neither then nor any minute of my life since. *The price we paid to become acquainted with God was a privilege to pay, and I am thankful that I was privileged to come in the Martin Handcart Company.*'"

After recounting this story in general conference, President James E. Faust taught,

Here, then, is a great truth. In the pain, the agony, and the heroic endeavors of life, we pass through a refiner's fire, and the insignificant and the unimportant in our lives can melt away like dross and make our faith bright, intact, and strong. In this way the divine image can be mirrored from the soul. It is part of the purging toll exacted of some to become acquainted with God. In the agonies of life, we seem to listen better to the faint, godly whisperings of the Divine Shepherd.[199]

As you conclude your study of the book of Job, consider how pain, for you, has been part of the "purging toll exacted" of you to "become acquainted with God."

---

199 President James E. Faust, "Refined in Our Trials," *Ensign*, February 2006, 3–4. See also "Pioneer Women," *Relief Society Magazine*, January 1948, 8.

AUGUST 8–14
"THE LORD IS MY SHEPHERD"
PSALMS 1–2; 8; 19–33; 40; 46

_____

God's Message to Me from This Section

_____

PSALMS 4–46—DISCOVERING DIVINITY IN MUSIC (20 MINUTES)

A significant part of the culture of the ancient Near East was music and song. Music was used for the purpose of celebrations, mourning, and expressing deep feelings of worship. What specific music do you use to

- Celebrate _____

- Mourn _____

- Worship _____

Music was an important part of the conversion of Alma the Younger and his close friend Ammon. They both testified of the power of singing "the song of redeeming love."[200] The word *Psalm* means "to praise" and is the Hebrew root for *hallelujah*, which specifically means "praise the Lord." Many Psalms are attributed to King David. Here are a few examples from the Psalms we are studying this week that are especially beautiful. As you read, highlight the ones that make your heart sing in praise to the Lord. If you are studying as a group, have each person pick their favorite *verse*. (Get it? *Verse* of scripture and *verse* of a song?)

- Psalms 4:4

- Psalms 8:3–5, 9

- Psalms 16:8–11

- Psalms 24:3–4

- Psalms 25:1

- Psalms 27:1

- Psalms 27:7

- Psalms 29:4

- Psalms 30:5

- Psalms 31:9

- Psalms 31:24

- Psalms 33:13–15

- Psalms 46:10

There is a popular modern psalm written about King David, which is intentionally called "Hallelujah." Below is a cover of this song performed by Pentatonix.

(or google "Hallelujah Pentatonix from A Pentatonix Christmas Special")

_____

200 See Alma 5:26 and Alma 26:8, 13. There are approximately twenty scriptural references to the importance of singing and music among the Book of Mormon people.

The purpose of your *Come, Follow Me* study over the next three weeks could be to find ways to praise the Lord through music. What constitutes music that helps us celebrate, mourn, and worship? I suppose if you asked fifty people, you would get about fifty different opinions. My principle for music comes from Moroni 7:13. As I apply it to music, it reads, "But behold, that [music] which is of God inviteth and enticeth to do good continually; wherefore, [music] which inviteth and enticeth to do good, and to love God, and to serve him, is inspired of God." In other words, *music that inspires me to love God and reach out to others in compassion, kindness, and patience is a personal psalm to me.* Here is one example.

(or google "What a Beautiful Name—Hillsong Worship BYU Vocal Point ft. David Archuleta")

This does not need to be limited to specific hymns of worship. Many of us have music we listen to that may not specifically talk about heaven, but its effects on us are heavenly. Can you think of some music that may fit this category for you?

PSALMS 23—MY PSALM OF REDEEMING LOVE (10 MINUTES)

Like so many other people, I would say Psalms 23 is my favorite. It expresses so many of my personal feelings in only six short verses. For example, early in our marriage, my wife and I would have experiences either individually or together that were so profound we struggled to adequately express them in words. For example, saying "I love you" after a while felt shallow and unrepresentative of the depth of our feelings. When we had each of our three kids, words could not adequately express the feelings we experienced. As we struggled to express the depth of our emotions, we read David's lyrics, "Thou anointest my head with oil; my cup runneth over. Surely goodness and mercy shall follow me all the days of my life" (Psalms 23:5–6). That simple hidden lyric, "*my cup runneth over,*" has become our song of deep expression. When each of our kids was born, *our cup runneth over.* As I dated

my wife, *my cup runneth over*. When my parents finally found hopeful and meaningful employment after years of struggle, *my cup runneth over*. When God has spoken to me in my dark places, *my cup runneth over*. Although life has its tragedies, it is vitally important to remember, protect, and save our *cup runneth over* moments. What are some *cup runneth over* moments for you and your family? Write a word or sentence about each one and list them in and around the cup below.

As you take the sacrament this coming Sunday, remember these moments you recorded. When the sacrament cup of water *runneth over* into your body, remember the role of Jesus Christ in these moments.

KNOWING THE WORDS, KNOWING THE SHEPHERD (5 MINUTES)

President Hugh B. Brown, a former member of the First Presidency, related this inspiring story:

> Some time ago a great actor in the city of New York gave a wonderful performance. There was thunderous applause at the end of the performance.

Some man in the audience thought he would like to hear this man read a scripture. He rose and said, "Sir, would you read for us the 23rd Psalm?"

Then the actor, being a great speaker as well as a great actor, said, "Why, yes, I know the words of the 23rd Psalm." And as such a man would read, he did read that wonderful psalm. When he finished, again there was thunderous applause.

But the actor arose and signaled for silence and said, "I appreciate your response, but there is a man sitting down here whom I happen to know. He is an elderly man. I would like for your benefit to have him come and really read the 23rd Psalm."

The old man, of course, was frightened, but he yielded to the invitation, staggered to the stand, and read as only such a man could read the 23rd Psalm. In quavering voice he said:

The Lord is my shepherd; I shall not want.

He maketh me to lie down in green pastures: he leadeth me beside the still waters.

He restoreth my soul: he leadeth me in the paths of righteousness for his name's sake.

Yea, though I walk through the valley of the shadow of death, I will fear no evil: for thou art with me; thy rod and thy staff they comfort me.

Thou preparest a table before me in the presence of mine enemies: thou anointest my head with oil; my cup runneth over.

Surely goodness and mercy shall follow me all the days of my life: and I will dwell in the house of the Lord for ever.

He sat down, and there was complete silence; many were wiping their eyes.

The great actor arose and said, "Ladies and gentlemen, as I told you, I know the *words* of the 23rd Psalm, but this man knows the *Shepherd*."

Oh, what a difference![201]

What are some things you know about Jesus Christ, not from scripture, not from someone else, but from your own personal experiences with Him?

---

201 "Father, Are You There?," BYU Devotional, October 8, 1967.

AUGUST 15–21

"I WILL DECLARE WHAT HE HATH DONE FOR MY SOUL"
PSALMS 49–51; 61–66; 69–72; 77–78; 85–86

God's Message to Me from This Section

PSALMS 51, 66, 69, 71, 85—WRITE YOUR OWN PSALM (20 MINUTES)

A great example of combining music with the gospel is in an inspirational message called "The Music of the Gospel." Go figure. After you watch this video, discuss what you think is the most important lesson the indigenous medicine man taught.

(or google "The Music of the Gospel")

Many psalms were written because David felt overwhelmed.[202] Sometimes it was because of his enemies, sometimes it was because he felt inadequate, sometimes it was because of his own sins, and many times it was because he simply wanted to connect with Jesus Christ. Here are some psalms you may want to turn to for comfort when you feel overwhelmed:

• Psalm 51: When I feel overwhelmed because of my own sins.

• Psalm 66: When I feel overwhelmed in my trials.

• Psalm 69: When I feel overwhelmed by loneliness. (This psalm is written from the perspective of a lonely Jesus looking for connection with His Father.)

• Psalm 71: When I feel overwhelmed because it seems that God is not there for me.

• Psalm 85: When I feel so overwhelmed that I'm not even sure where to start.

World famous songwriter Paul McCartney talked about an unforgettable dream he had at the age of twenty-four. He told about how his mother, Mary, appeared to him ten years after she had passed away from breast cancer. The point of her visit was to convey a message to her son when he felt overwhelmed and troubled: *Let it be!* I don't think it's much of a stretch to consider this song a psalm for Paul.

Take a few minutes to write your own psalm that can help you when you feel overwhelmed. It doesn't need to be poetic, and it doesn't need to be long, but it does need to be authentic to you. I have found that most of us need between five and ten verses to adequately write a meaningful psalm. For me, it is useful to start with simple lines from scriptures or hymns. Good luck!

---

202 See Psalms 55:5; 61:2; 77:3; 142:3; 143:4.

AUGUST 22–28
"LET EVERY THING THAT HATH BREATH PRAISE THE LORD"
PSALMS 102–103; 110; 116–119; 127–128; 135–139; 146–150

God's Message to Me from This Section

THE IMPACT OF PSALMS ON JESUS CHRIST (20 MINUTES)

Elder Jeffrey R. Holland of the Quorum of the Twelve Apostles said, "Jesus Himself quoted the book of Psalms more than any other Old Testament text. Beyond the Savior's own use of these writings, the authors of the four Gospels [Matthew, Mark, Luke, and John] drew heavily on the psalms as they strove to document His life and ministry, particularly those excruciating hours of His arrest, trial, and Crucifixion."[203]

If you haven't already noticed, many psalms are written *messianically*, meaning they are written from the perspective of Jesus Christ. It is almost as if He wrote them Himself. David and Isaiah wrote messianically more than anyone else in the Old Testament. Many of these instances describe personal details of the Savior's mortal ministry, suffering, and atoning sacrifice.

Elder James E. Talmage taught the following about the development of the Christ child.

> [Jesus] came among men to experience all the natural conditions of mortality; He was born as truly a dependent,

helpless babe as is any other child; His infancy was in all common features as the infancy of others; His boyhood was actual boyhood, His development was as necessary and as real as that of all children. *Over His mind had fallen the veil of forgetfulness common to all who are born to earth, by which the remembrance of [premortal] existence is shut off.* The Child grew, and with growth there came to Him expansion of mind, development of faculties, and progression in power and understanding. His advancement was from one grace to another.[204]

Jesus had to rediscover who He was as He grew up. How did He figure it out? It's clear that much of His early self-discovery was revealed to Him as He read Psalms and Isaiah. Because of this, one of my favorite questions as I read many of the psalms is, *I wonder what these meant to Jesus during the early part of His life?* David wrote the book of Psalms as if *he* were the Savior, so there must be value in reading them as if *we* are.

Here are some examples of what Jesus may have learned about Himself from the book of Psalms. In my mind, I picture the first two columns as an entry in His personal

---

203 *For Times of Trouble: Spiritual Solace from the Psalms* [2012], 7–8. See also *Old Testament Seminary Teacher Manual,* "Lesson 110: Psalms, Part 1," (Church Educational System manual, 2015).

204 *Jesus the Christ* [1981], 111–112; emphasis added.

scripture journal as a kid and the last column to track when the psalms were fulfilled throughout His life.

2:7	I am the only Begotten of the Father	Matthew 3:17; John 3:16
8:2	I will be praised by children	Matthew 21:15–16
16:10	I will rise from the dead	Matthew 28:7
22:1	I will be forsaken by my Father	Matthew 27:46
22:16	My feet and hands will be pierced	John 20:27
34:20	My bones shall not be broken	John 19:32–33, 36
41:9	A friend I know and trust will betray me	Luke 22:47
68:18	I will ascend into heaven	Acts 1:9–11
109:8	I will pray for my enemies	Matthew 7:44; Luke 23:34
118:22	I am the Chief Cornerstone	Matthew 21:42; Ephesians 2:20
118:26	I come in the name of the Father	Matthew 21:9

Can you think of scriptures that reveal to you who you are and how we can fulfill our specific missions on Earth? This could be a good place to start.

Romans 8:16	I am a literal child of God with divine identity and eternal potential	
Ephesians 4:11–13	Christ has a church and a ministry for me	

Matthew 28:18–20	My ministry is to gather Israel	
Mosiah 18:8–10	My covenants teach me to mourn, comfort, and stand as a witness	

PSALMS 113–118—INFINITE COMFORT (15 MINUTES)

After the Last Supper and just before Gethsemane, Matthew 26:30 explains, "They had sung an hymn, [and then] they went out into the mount of Olives." It is clear from scripture that Jesus knew exactly what was about to happen. He knew what was going to happen in Gethsemane that night. He knew He would be tried and tortured later that night, and crucified the next day. Pause! What hymn would you turn to if you were in desperate need of comfort? Read or sing the lyrics and write down your three favorite lines or words.

Hymn name _____

Three favorite lines or words:

1. _____

2. _____

3. _____

Discuss: This hymn brings me comfort because . . .

Because all of this happened to Jesus during the week of Passover, we can assume the hymns Jesus sang to bring comfort and calm were attached to this celebration of deliverance: "The 'hymn' the Savior and His disciples sang at the conclusion of the Last Supper was probably the traditional Jewish recitation from Psalms 113–118, called the *Hallel*. Psalms 113–114 were traditionally sung at the beginning of the meal, and Psalms 115–118 were traditionally sung as part of the formal closing of a Passover meal."[205]

As you read Psalms 113–118, mark the lyrics to the *Hallel* that you think would have been most comforting to Jesus and His Apostles. Now imagine you were there in this sacred yet scary moment and do the same activity above: find your three favorite lines or words and write them down.

Hymn Name: The *Hallel* (Psalms 113–118)

Three favorite lines or words:

1. _____

2. _____

3. _____

Discuss: The *Hallel* brings me comfort because . . .

Let's end our study of the book of Psalms with Psalm 118:14: "The Lord is my strength and song, and is become my salvation." As you look back on the last three weeks of study, what strength have you experienced because of the book of Psalms?

---

205 *New Testament Student Manual,* "Lesson 9: Matthew 26," [2018].

AUGUST 29–SEPTEMBER 4
"THE FEAR OF THE LORD IS THE BEGINNING OF WISDOM"
PROVERBS 1–4; 15–16; 22; 31; ECCLESIASTES 1–3; 11–12

God's Message to Me from This Section

SWITCH IT UP (15 MINUTES)

I had a student once describe Proverbs as a book of ancient inspirational memes. In a way, she's right. Proverbs primarily consists of important wisdom from ancient Israel, much of which is attributed to King Solomon. So, as you study Proverbs and Ecclesiastes this week, my purpose is to give you a simple method and see where it takes you.

Before we start, there is one important clarification I want to make. Proverbs 1:7 teaches, "The fear of the Lord is the beginning of knowledge: but fools despise wisdom and instruction." The phrase "fear of the Lord" is repeated in Proverbs seventeen times in thirty-one chapters. Therefore, it is vital to understand what this phrase means and what it does *not* mean. Biblical scholar Kerry Muhlestein explained:

> This phrase [the fear of the Lord] contrasts the ability to gain wisdom and knowledge by learning through the fear of the Lord with the foolishness that results when we don't. . . .
>
> Fearing the Lord is an important theme throughout the Old Testament, yet Latter-day Saints shy away from the idea. . . . While the Old Testament's dominant theme is that of a loving and

forgiving God who continually extends opportunities for forgiveness, it balances that with a powerful God who should be both loved and feared. . . .

> What we must fear is the punishment that God will bring upon us as His way of bringing us back to Him when we stray outside our covenants. *We create a false god in our minds if we imagine a God whose correcting measures should not be feared.*

He concludes:

> These measures are for our good and are born out of love, but they are difficult and we should fear to invite them. The scriptures teach that we must fear God and that in doing so we will learn His ways and love Him all the more. This theme is superbly taught in Proverbs.[206]

Write each of the following on a piece of paper and then cut or tear them out so they are individual. Now fold them in half twice and put them in a bowl. Each day before your study, have someone close their eyes and draw a slip of paper from the bowl. Whatever you draw is how you will study for that day.

---

206 Kerry Muhlestein, *The Essential Old Testament Companion* (Covenant Communications, 2013), 346–47; emphasis added.

BACKWARD OBJECT LESSONS

Choose two or three objects in your home before you read. While reading, see if you can find principles that can be taught using your objects.

MEMORIZE

Find an important verse or phrase and memorize it. Add specific actions so that instead of simply repeating it, you perform the verse.

IF I WERE THE KING/QUEEN

Pick two or three principles from what you read that you would use to lead a kingdom.

SONG OR VIDEO

As you read today, try to find a song or video online that corresponds with something you read.

DRAW A PICTURE

Draw a picture that could represent an important principle you read. Remember to color it and share it!

TOP 5 LISTS

As you read today, come up with a "top 5 most useful wisdom" list. You could also come up with a "top 5 most confusing verses" list. Can you come up with any other top 5 lists?

SEPTEMBER 5–11
"GOD IS MY SALVATION"
ISAIAH 1–12

God's Message to Me from This Section

WORD CLOUD! (10 MINUTES)

A word cloud is a useful visual way of recognizing repetition and themes in certain text. The larger the word, the more it is used. I created the following word cloud using all sixty-six chapters in the book of Isaiah.[207] Most words you see are repeated at least fifty times. For

example, the word most often used by Isaiah is *Lord*, at 476 times! Because these words are out of context, there are inherent limitations to studying this way. But it is still instructive to see what Isaiah is continually focused on. What do you notice simply by analyzing Isaiah's words in this way?

207 Created using worditout.com.

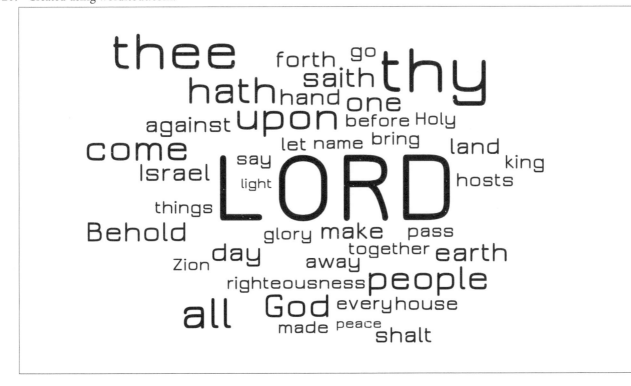

I notice *attributes of Christ*, such as glory, light, holy, peace, righteousness, king.

I notice *big-picture* words, such as Israel, Zion, all, every, earth.

I notice *relationship* words, such as come, together, bring, one, house, name.

Pick two to three words from the word cloud that you want to learn more about as you read Isaiah.

ISAIAH 1–2; 6—KEEP IT SIMPLE (10 MINUTES)

To introduce why he is duplicating some of the words of Isaiah, Nephi taught:

> Behold, my soul delighteth in proving unto my people the truth of the coming of **Christ**; for, for this end hath the law of Moses been given; and all things which have been given of God from the beginning of the world, unto man, are the typifying of him.
>
> And also my soul delighteth in the **covenants** of the Lord which he hath made to our fathers; yea, my soul delighteth in his **grace**, and in his **justice**, and **power**, and **mercy** in **the great and eternal plan of deliverance from death**.
>
> And my soul delighteth in proving unto my people that save **Christ should come** all men must perish (2 Nephi 11:4–6; emphasis added).

Nephi identified at least three themes to look for when searching the words of Isaiah. They are:

• Christ (His mercy, grace, justice, and power)

• Covenants

• Current and coming events

A simple way to identify these themes is by reading the chapter headings. If you can identify the important themes before you read each chapter, it will help you find meaning and clarity even if you don't understand everything. Here are a couple of examples:

Covenant

ISAIAH 1

The people of Israel are apostate, rebellious, and corrupt; only a few remain faithful—The people's sacrifices and feasts are rejected—They are called upon to repent and work righteousness—Zion will be redeemed in the day of restoration.

Coming Events

Coming Events **Coming Events** **Coming Events**

ISAIAH 2

Isaiah sees the latter-day temple, gathering of Israel, and millennial judgment and peace—The proud and wicked will be brought low at the Second Coming—Compare 2 Nephi 12.

Coming Events **Coming Events**

Christ **Christ**

ISAIAH 6

Isaiah sees the Lord—His sins are forgiven—He is called to prophesy—He prophesies of the Jews' rejection of Christ's teachings—A remnant will return—Compare 2 Nephi 16.

Coming Events

ISAIAH 6—GET OUT YOUR SHOVEL. LET'S DIG DEEP! (15 MINUTES)

Isaiah 6 includes Isaiah's vision of Jesus Christ and a beautifully vulnerable Isaiah. It is richly symbolic and widely relevant to what it's like to be mortal. Moses taught, and the Doctrine and Covenants confirms, that the purpose of temples is to provide a clear path to the presence of God.[208] This is the ultimate effect of covenant keeping in eternity, but it is also an invitation to enjoy a fulfilling relationship with God in mortality. Isaiah begins by seeing the Lord in the temple. A brief look back at the symbolism of the tabernacle and temple adds richness and relevance to this experience.

---

208 See Exodus 19:11 (5–11); 32:19 (19–29); Deuteronomy 4:14; 30:11 (11–14); D&C 84:20–23 (18–24).

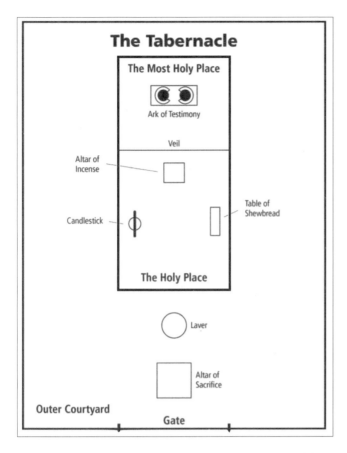

The Tabernacle

The Most Holy Place

Ark of Testimony

Veil

Altar of Incense

Candlestick

Table of Shewbread

The Holy Place

Laver

Altar of Sacrifice

Outer Courtyard

Gate

The *Outer Courtyard* represents the telestial world, or the world in which we now live. This worldly experience makes it difficult to feel and see the Savior's influence in our lives. To draw closer to Christ, we must choose to sacrifice and be born again, thus taking upon us the name of Jesus Christ. This commitment speaks to our desire to choose a relationship with Christ over telestial pleasures and outcomes. Sacrifice and rebirth become who we are. The lifestyle we live, which is intended to deepen our relationship with Christ, is described in detail in Mosiah 18:8–10.

The *Holy Place* represents the terrestrial world. Scripture often refers to the people here as Zion.[209] They live by the light of the Holy Spirit (candlestick), and they are sustained by the Bread of Life (table of shewbread). For us, this is an obvious connection to the sacrament ordinance as well as our endowment experience. Because we choose to live by the Spirit, we allow Him to reveal the character and personality of Jesus to us in deeply personal ways. Our hearts are becoming one with Christ as we learn from our own experience what it feels like to be

found by the Good Shepherd.[210] The Good Shepherd sustains us, feeds us, cares for us, and protects us through His loving grace.

The *Most Holy Place* represents the celestial world. The only furniture here is the ark of the covenant, or mercy seat, representing the presence and throne of God. Each must pass through the veil. On the veil and surrounding the ark are cherubim, or angels. As each person passes through the veil, they must also pass these angels, who stand as sentinels, or guardians, to the presence of God. The Lord described this experience and invitation to Moses: "And there I will meet with thee, and I will commune with thee from above the mercy seat, from between the two cherubims which are upon the ark of the testimony, of all things which I will give thee in commandment unto the children of Israel."[211]

Elder Richard G. Scott's favorite scripture was Omni 1:26. This verse has served as a one-verse reminder of the purpose and path taught in the temple: "And now, my beloved brethren, I would that ye should come unto Christ, who is the Holy One of Israel, and partake of his salvation, and the power of his redemption. Yea, come unto him, and offer your whole souls as an offering unto him, and continue in fasting and praying, and endure to the end; and as the Lord liveth ye will be saved."

To this, I would add Doctrine and Covenants 93:1: "Verily, thus saith the Lord: It shall come to pass that every soul who forsaketh his sins and cometh unto me, and calleth on my name, and obeyeth my voice, and keepeth my commandments, shall see my face and know that I am."

As we approach Isaiah 6, imagine yourself as if you are Isaiah. Refer to this table for basic meanings to the symbolism in verses 1–6.

1	"His train filled the temple"	The power, authority, and influence of Jesus Christ

209 See D&C 97:8, 15–16, 21; Moses 7:18.

210 Notice the consistent message of temple symbolism with John 10:2–16. Christ's sheep enter in by the door, hearken to the voice of the Shepherd, and ignore the voice of strangers. Christ's sheep know they are protected by the Shepherd because He gave His life for them.

211 Exodus 25:22; see also Doctrine and Covenants 132:19.

2	Wings of the seraphims	Their power to act and move in obedience to God's will (see Doctrine and Covenants 77:4)
4	Posts shake, the temple is filled with smoke	When Jehovah was on Mt. Sinai the mountain shook and there was smoke as He reestablished His covenant with His people (see Exodus 19). The Lord is clearly testifying, "I am here."
6	Hot coal from the altar that purged Isaiah's weakness and inadequacy.	We aren't sure if this coal is from the altar of incense or the altar of sacrifice. When a lamb was offered on the altar of sacrifice, its blood would drip down on the hot coals and extinguish the flames. This taught that through Christ's blood, He can extinguish our guilt, pain, inadequacy, and brokenness. If Isaiah was at the altar of incense, a similar principle could be taught because the hot coals from the altar of sacrifice were placed on the altar of incense each morning. At the altar of incense, smoke would rise like prayers going to heaven. At times, prayers would be offered by uplifted hands (see Revelation 8:3–4; Psalm 141:1).

Here are some questions and points to ponder as you internalize Isaiah's experience and make it your own.

- When Isaiah stands before the Lord and experiences the Lord's power in a vision in verse 5, what

is Isaiah's immediate reaction? (*Undone* in Hebrew means "cut off"; he was overwhelmed by his consciousness of his and his people's sins).[212]

- In verse 6–7, how does the Savior respond to Isaiah's feelings of inadequacy? How *doesn't* the Savior respond?

- In verse 8, how does this personal experience with the grace, mercy, and love of Christ change Isaiah's confidence in himself? How does it change Isaiah's confidence, or trust, in the Lord?

- What are some things we learn about the character of Jesus Christ and how He handles our feelings of fear and inadequacy?

- Identify a situation where you simply don't feel like you measure up to what God wants. Imagine you could express your struggles to Isaiah. What do you think Isaiah would say to you to bring you hope?

- How does Isaiah's response in verse 8, "Here am I; send me," show a devotion and understanding of the mission of Jesus Christ?[213]

ISAIAH 6:5—"WOE IS ME! FOR I AM UNDONE" (10 MINUTES)

Watch the following video and look for two things:

1. What are all the similarities you can find between Drew's story and Isaiah's story?

2. What does Drew discover regarding Jesus Christ through his journey?

(or google "I Didn't Feel Good Enough, But I Was Good Enough for God, His Grace")

What have you learned about the character of Christ by studying Isaiah's vision? How does an understanding of who Christ is influence your desire to make and keep covenants?

---

212 See Isaiah 6:5a.
213 See Abraham 3:22–27.

SEPTEMBER 12–18
"A MARVELLOUS WORK AND A WONDER"
ISAIAH 13–14; 24–30; 35

God's Message to Me from This Section

YOU'VE GOT THIS! (2 MINUTES)

The themes in this week's chapters are much more familiar and clear to members of The Church of Jesus Christ of Latter-day Saints because they are about the latter days! These chapters are heavily focused on the problem presented by a global scattering of Israel and the solutions the Lord has in the last days. These solutions are what the Lord calls a "marvellous work and a wonder."[214] This marvellous work and a wonder includes the coming forth of the Book of Mormon, the restoration of the gospel, a global gathering of Israel to temples, difficulties and tragedies leading up to the Second Coming of Jesus Christ, and the eventual promise of millennial peace and rest. As both a seer and personal witness of the Lord Jesus Christ, Isaiah pleads with Israel to remember their divine nature and move forward to their eternal inheritance.

ISAIAH 13–35—WHAT'S IN A NAME? (15 MINUTES)

Do you know what your name means? Why were you given your name? Does the meaning of your name represent you? If you could change your name, what would you change it to and why?

Isaiah used the names of two of his sons to teach an obsession he had with the scattering and gathering of Israel. As a seer, it was almost as if he couldn't stop seeing it! In Isaiah 8:1, 3, he introduced *Maher-shalal-hash-baz.* This name means "to speed to the spoil, he hasteneth the prey." In a word, this name means to *scatter.* Isaiah 7:3 tells us the name of the other son, *Shear-jashub.* His name means "the remnant shall return." In a word, this name means to *gather.* Isaiah then testifies, "Behold, I and the children whom the Lord hath given me are for signs and for wonders in Israel from the Lord of hosts, which dwelleth in mount Zion."[215] Although these may not be their literal names, Isaiah at least identifies them this way to emphasize the importance of the gathering and scattering of Israel both on a local and global scale.

Read the chapter headings below, and identify if the specific chapter is about *Maher-shalal-hash-baz* (scattering), *Shear-jashub* (gathering), or both.

- Isaiah 13 _____
- Isaiah 14 _____
- Isaiah 24 _____
- Isaiah 25 _____
- Isaiah 26 _____
- Isaiah 27 _____

214 Isaiah 29:14.

215 Isaiah 8:18.

- Isaiah 28 _____
- Isaiah 29 _____
- Isaiah 30 _____
- Isaiah 35 _____

ISAIAH 13–35—*RESTORATION* IS NOT A WORD ABOUT EVENTS; IT IS AN ATTRIBUTE OF JESUS CHRIST (15 MINUTES)

Ask any group of Latter-day Saints to describe to you what *the Restoration* is and you will get answers about Joseph Smith, the First Vision, the Book of Mormon, priesthood, temples, the gathering of Israel, etc. Although these are *evidence* of the Restoration, they are not the core of this eternally significant attribute of Jesus Christ. Without Jesus Christ, all the events of the Restoration have no actual restoring power. Without Jesus Christ, the events of the Restoration are meaningless, hopeless, powerless, and futile.

Jesus Christ, by His very nature, is the Restorer. Jesus Christ restores life, He restores hope, He restores peace, and, ultimately, He restores us back to our heavenly home. All of the *evidence* of the Restoration points back to the *restoring* power of Jesus Christ. Each testifies of Him in significant ways. As you read about the events happening in the last days in these chapters, consider this formula to refocus on the true Restorer.

In what ways does _____ testify of the restoring power of Jesus Christ?

You can fill in the blank with things such as the gathering of Israel, the Book of Mormon, revelation through living prophets, the Second Coming and Millennium, the building of Zion, etc.

In conclusion, discuss or write down events of the Restoration that have drawn you to Jesus Christ in very real ways.

SEPTEMBER 19–25
"COMFORT YE MY PEOPLE"
ISAIAH 40–49

God's Message to Me from This Section

ISAIAH 22:20–25—"A NAIL IN THE SURE PLACE" (10 MINUTES)

An additional obsession Isaiah had is the temple. The temple is a symbolic representation that Jesus Christ's deepest desire is to gather *all* the children of our Heavenly Parents back to Their presence. In Isaiah 22:22–25, we get a very useful temple teaching. In this chapter, Isaiah refers to an obscure story of when Shebna, who held a high position in King Hezekiah's court, abused his power. Eliakim replaced Shebna and was trusted with the "key of the house of David." Eliakim's name means "God shall cause to arise,"[216] and Isaiah uses him as a type for Christ. In this context, Isaiah taught, "And I will fasten him as *a nail in a sure place*; and he shall be for a glorious throne to his father's house. And they shall hang upon him all the glory of his father's house. . . . In that day, saith the Lord of hosts, shall *the nail that is fastened in the sure place* be removed, and be cut down, and fall; and the burden that was upon it shall be cut off: for the Lord hath spoken it."[217] Elder Jeffrey R. Holland commented on these verses:

> When the Roman soldiers drove their four-and-one-half-inch crucifixion spikes into their victim's flesh, they did so first in the open palm. But because the weight of the body might tear that flesh and not sustain the burden to be carried, they also drove nails into the wrist, down the nexus of bones and sinews that would not tear no matter what the weight. Thus, the nail in the wrist was the "nail in the sure place."

> Once it was removed and the Savior was "cut down," the burden of the crucified body (more literally, the burden of the Atonement) was brought to an end. In terms of our salvation, Christ is the Nail in a Sure Place—never failing, never faltering.[218]

Now let's warm our hands by the fire of Isaiah's faith in Jesus Christ. As you read these scriptures about the Savior, think about how Jesus Christ will never fail, never falter, and will become the Nail in the Sure Place for you.

- Isaiah 1:18
- Isaiah 9:6–7

---

216 See Isaiah 22:20 footnote a.
217 Isaiah 22:23–25; emphasis added.
218 *Witness for His Names* (Deseret Book Company, 2019), 113. For a more in-depth understanding of the "nail in the sure place," see John Hilton III, *Considering the Cross* (Deseret Book Company, 2021), 46–57.

- Isaiah 40:1–2
- Isaiah 40:31
- Isaiah 41:10–13
- Isaiah 42:6–7
- Isaiah 43:1–7
- Isaiah 44:22–24
- Isaiah 46:3–4
- Isaiah 49:14–16

ISAIAH 49:14–16—"I HAVE GRAVEN THEE UPON THE PALMS OF MY HANDS" (15 MINUTES)

As you read Isaiah 49:14–16, consider the emotion and stillness of Isaiah as he wrote them. What was he feeling? Did he have his wife, the prophetess,[219] in mind? As you meditate on this, watch these two videos about the love of Christ sung by different choirs.

(or google "Because He Lives (Amen) West Coast Choir")

(or google "I Feel My Savior's Love, Sweet Is the Work")

The deeply personal and painful imagery in Isaiah 22 of the nail in the sure place adds depth to the Savior's testimony in Isaiah 49:14–16. Interestingly, to testify to us again of His reliability and love, He invokes another painful and personal image—that of a loving, committed mother giving birth to a child. Of this declaration Elder Jeffrey R. Holland testified: "No love in mortality comes closer to approximating the pure love of Jesus Christ than the selfless love a devoted mother has for her child. When Isaiah . . . wanted to convey Jehovah's love, he invoked the image of a mother's devotion. 'Can a woman forget her sucking child?' he asks. How absurd, he implies, though not as absurd as thinking Christ will ever forget us."[220]

Here is an additional witness from Elder Holland regarding the loving hands of Jesus Christ.

(or google "Holland, We Are Graven on the Palms of His Hands")

As you discuss the following question, notice that it is phrased from the Savior's perspective, not yours.

When Jesus looks at His hands and thinks of you, how do you think He really feels?

---

219   Isaiah 8:3.

220   "Behold Thy Mother," *Ensign*, November 2015, 48.

SEPTEMBER 26–OCTOBER 2
"HE HATH BORNE OUR GRIEFS, AND CARRIED OUR SORROWS"
ISAIAH 50–57

God's Message to Me from This Section

ISAIAH 52–53—WHY STUDY THE SUFFERING CHRIST? (20 MINUTES)

The very center of my personal witness of Jesus Christ focuses on His suffering. In my opinion, Isaiah 50–53 teaches Christ's suffering more beautifully and poetically than any other place in the Old Testament. Abinadi was so captivated by Isaiah's words, he included them in his sermon to King Noah and his wicked priests with the purpose of helping them "apply their hearts to understanding."[221]

Studying scriptural descriptions of the Crucifixion and suffering of Jesus Christ can have a lasting impact on our souls. BYU Professor of Religion John Hilton III taught about the purpose of studying the suffering Christ:

> The fact that the Savior died for me and for you brings a special intimacy to our relationship with him. When we understand the personal nature of Jesus's sacrifice, his Atonement becomes a one-on-one experience between the Savior and each of us. He knows us and wants us to know him. Christ hung on the cross—not to make us feel bad, but to make us feel good. His death is a tender and personal sacrifice for us, and

our acceptance of his sacrifice can be just as tender and personal to him.[222]

Studying the suffering Christ helps bring a one-on-one intimacy between us and our Savior that will leave a deep, lasting mark on us just as it did on Him.

In Isaiah 52:1–3, Isaiah talks about how we undervalue our worth. He says, "Ye have sold yourselves for nought," but then promises that we "shall be redeemed without money"—redeemed with something far more valuable than money: the body and blood of Jesus Christ. Isaiah 53:3–5 continues with intimate specificity, "[Jesus] is despised and rejected of men; a man of sorrows, and acquainted with grief: and we hid as it were our faces from him; he was despised, and we esteemed him not. Surely he hath borne our griefs, and carried our sorrows: yet we did esteem him stricken, smitten of God, and afflicted. But he was wounded for our transgressions, he was bruised for our iniquities: the chastisement of our peace was upon him; and with his stripes we are healed."

As I mentioned in the lesson for May 9–15, which covered Numbers 21, one way we know what something is worth is by analyzing the investment, or price paid, for the thing. The price paid for your soul and mine was the

---

221 See Mosiah 12:26–27; Mosiah 14.

222 John Hilton III, *Considering the Cross* (Deseret Book Company, 2021), 92.

life and death of the infinite Christ. This testifies that we are all worth saving! As we study, foster, and rely on the suffering Christ, we not only come to know Him, but we also come to know ourselves. As we study the suffering Christ, we undervalue ourselves less and come to know Him more. As you watch these videos, pray and ask God to witness to you that you are also worth saving. He may not answer right away, but He will answer!

(or google "None Were with Him—An Apostle's Easter Thoughts on Christ")

(or google "BYU Noteworthy: Come Thou Fount of Every Blessing")

(or google "Be Still, My Soul—Music Video The Church of Jesus Christ of Latter-day Saints")

Can you think of one example from scripture where Jesus Christ helped someone see the worth of their soul?

Because your soul is worth saving, so is the soul of every other person you will ever meet!

ISAIAH 55:8–9—GOD SEES THE END FROM THE BEGINNING (10 MINUTES)

To help you understand this attribute of Jesus Christ a little better, watch the video of Dieter F. Uchtdorf as he tells the story where he almost didn't become a fighter pilot. (Gasp!) Notice how Jesus saw far more in young Dieter than he could ever see in himself. Also notice how this story begins with a very inconvenient move for the Uchtdorf family. (Only watch from time code 1:20–5:13)

(or google "Dieter F. Uchtdorf See the End from the Beginning")

As you look back on some of your life experiences, what evidence can you see that testifies to you that you can trust in God's ability to see the end from the beginning?

OCTOBER 3–9
"THE REDEEMER SHALL COME TO ZION"
ISAIAH 58–66

_____

God's Message to Me from This Section

_____

ISAIAH 61—MISSION STATEMENTS (15 MINUTES)

Match the mission statements to which major company you think they belong to.

Mission Statements

A. "Bring inspiration and innovation to every athlete* in the world." (*if you have a body, you are an athlete)

B. "Save people money so they can live better."

C. "To bring the best user experience to its customers through its innovative hardware, software, and services."

D. "To glorify God by being a faithful steward of all that is entrusted to us. To have a positive influence on all who come in contact with [us]."

E. "Our mission is to empower every person and every organization on the planet to achieve more."

F. "To devote its talent and technology to creating superior products and services that contribute to a better global society."

G. "Our mission is to make delicious feel-good moments easy for everyone."

Companies

1. Chick-fil-A _____

2. Nike _____

3. Microsoft _____

4. Samsung _____

5. McDonald's _____

6. Apple _____

7. Walmart _____

(Answers: Chick-fil-a, D; Nike, A; Microsoft, E; Samsung, F; McDonald's, G; Apple, C; Walmart, B)

I'm not sure if Jesus has a formal mission statement, but if He did, what would it say? Take a few minutes to write a mission statement for Jesus in three sentences or fewer.

The mission of Jesus Christ is _____

_____

_____

_____.

Near the beginning of His mortal ministry, Jesus was preaching in Nazareth. Nazareth was a small town of 600–800 people, so everyone would have probably known everyone. Plus, it was where Mary grew up. A young Jesus running around the streets of Nazareth would have been a common occurrence. But this time was different. Now fully grown, He went to the synagogue on the Sabbath day and stood up to read. What occurred next was nothing short of shocking to those in attendance. Jesus read out loud Isaiah 61:1–2. At the end, He openly testified, "This day is this scripture fulfilled in your ears" (see Luke 4:16–21). What does it say that caused such an uproar? To me, this is the mission statement of Jesus Christ (I will add v.3):

> The Spirit of the Lord God is upon me; because the Lord hath anointed me to preach good tidings unto the meek; he hath sent me to bind up the brokenhearted, to proclaim liberty to the captives, and the opening of the prison to them that are bound;
>
> To proclaim the acceptable year of the Lord, and the day of vengeance of our God; to comfort all that mourn;
>
> To appoint unto them that mourn in Zion, to give unto them beauty for ashes, the oil of joy for mourning, the garment of praise for the spirit of heaviness; that they might be called trees of righteousness, the planting of the Lord, that he might be glorified.

If I were writing this as a mission statement, I might write:

> *"The mission of Jesus Christ is to preach good tidings to the meek, bind up the brokenhearted, liberate prisoners and captives, preach the acceptable year of the Lord, replace ashes with beauty, replace mourning with joy, and replace heaviness with the garment of praise, all to glorify God."*

Based on these verses, who is Jesus specifically searching for? The meek, broken, prisoners, captives, those in ashes, those who mourn and are experiencing heavy burdens. Let me ask the same question in a more personal way: Based on these verses, is Jesus looking for you? Is He looking for your kids? Your friends? And when He finds us, what are His intentions with all of us?

What do these verses tell you about the character of Jesus Christ?

Do you have a personal witness of the mission statement of Jesus Christ? In what ways do you choose to attach yourself to His promises?

DEBRIEF ISAIAH (10 MINUTES)

In the following box, write some of the things you learned and experienced while studying Isaiah over the past five weeks. If you have teenagers studying with you, have them come up with three to five hashtags that capture what they learned from Isaiah. If you have small children, invite them to color a picture of something that came up in your Isaiah studies.

OCTOBER 10–16
"BEFORE I FORMED THEE IN THE BELLY I KNEW THEE"
JEREMIAH 1–3; 7; 16–18; 20

God's Message to Me from This Section

JEREMIAH 20—IT'S BETTER WHEN ELDER HOLLAND SAYS IT (10 MINUTES)

It is no secret that Jeremiah's forty years of preaching were hard. Not only were they hard, but he also witnessed major devastation among his people as Babylon conquered Jerusalem. Most Old Testament scripture focuses on the word of the Lord revealed to prophets. Jeremiah is different because we also read about his insecurities, frustrations, and desires to quit. He wanted to help far more than he was able, and because of his authenticity, there are many aspects of his ministry that are relevant and applicable today.

In June 2021, Elder Holland spoke at the seminar for new mission leaders. He used the vulnerability of Jeremiah in his talk to teach powerful truths that could validate inadequacies of missionaries and give them strength to keep going. Elder Holland said, "After being called somewhat against his will, the Old Testament prophet Jeremiah's mission went from bad to worse. Finally, he was thrown into jail. 'O Lord, thou hast deceived me,' Jeremiah said. 'I was deceived: . . . I am in derision daily, every one mocketh me. . . . I will not make mention of [thee], nor speak any more in [thy] name.'"[223]

Elder Holland then added his own modern flair to Jeremiah's feelings:

"You didn't tell me anything about jail time, Lord. I went back through my notes from the mission leadership seminar, and there was not one word about handcuffs and incarceration. . . .

"I have told my last account of the First Vision. I am not handing out another pass-along card, and I am unfriending everyone except perhaps my children on my Facebook page. I am through, I am done, I am finished, kaput."

Then, in spite of rejection, homesickness, "rainy days and Dear John letters and opposition in all things," Jeremiah uttered a telling line: "But his word was in mine heart as a burning fire shut up in my bones, and I [grew] weary with forbearing, and I could not stay."[224]

"What kept him in the harness?" Elder Holland asked. "What kept him from going home? What makes a missionary get up on time, love every companion,

---

223 Jeremiah 20:7, 9.

224 Jeremiah 20:9.

work hard early and late, trying to be the best he or she can be every day of that mission?"

The answer—"The Words of Christ."[225]

Now go back and mark all the verses Elder Holland quotes. You may even want to link them together in your Gospel Library app.

Jeremiah 1:5–7 🔗 Jeremiah 20:7, 9

What scriptures are in your heart "as a burning fire shut up in [your] bones"?

A major part of serving a mission for me was wrestling with significant depression. At the time, I did not know what it was. I knew it wasn't homesickness, and I knew it wasn't physical sickness, but there lay a thick darkness over my emotions and spirit almost all the time. In fact, there were more nights than I can count that I would wait for my companion to go to bed and then I would go out to our small living room and cry myself to sleep.

About halfway through my mission, I found a scripture that made all the difference. This scripture was the last verse from a prominent prophet who spent months unfairly imprisoned. His people were suffering, and he felt helpless. Many of the verses before reflected his broken heart. The Lord's words to him reflected genuine validation, peace, and comfort. Of course, I'm speaking of Joseph Smith in Liberty Jail. Still, in the darkness of the jail, Joseph Smith declared: "Therefore, dearly beloved brethren, let us cheerfully do all things that lie in our power; and then may we stand still, with the utmost assurance, to see the salvation of God, and for his arm to be revealed."[226]

This scripture instantly lit a fire in my bones! I memorized it, knowing that if Joseph had tried to be positive in prison, I could do my best in my circumstances as well. Serving a mission became less about doing everything and more about cheerfully doing what was in my power each day. Many days, there was no cheer, so I attempted to simply be less sad. I still cried late at night at times, but I felt like Jesus was there for me. He accepted me.

He inspired me. He brought me enough peace to calm my troubled heart. I still think about this verse all the time.

JEREMIAH 7:1–7—B.T.T.Y. (10 MINUTES)

In 2019, President Russell M. Nelson spoke about repentance. As part of his talk, he taught us Greek: "The word for *repentance* in the Greek New Testament is *metanoeo*. The prefix *meta-* means 'change.' The suffix *-noeo* is related to Greek words that mean 'mind,' 'knowledge,' 'spirit,' and 'breath.' Thus, when Jesus asks you and me to 'repent,' He is inviting us to change our mind, our knowledge, our spirit—even the way we breathe. He is asking us to change the way we love, think, serve, spend our time, treat our wives, teach our children, and even care for our bodies."[227]

A common misconception about repentance is that it causes suffering. It does not! The Savior clearly taught that we can choose to "repent *or* suffer."[228] Repentance is less about trying to avoid punishment and more about trying to access potential. It is less about avoiding damnation and more about changing our disposition. It is less about checking boxes, and more about changing our breath.

Jeremiah's people were covetous, unwilling to listen, and grievous revolters.[229] Therefore, he invites them to "stand in the gate of the Lord's house" and "amend your ways and your doings."[230] The Lord then gives three *if* and one *then* for them to consider.

> For *if* ye thoroughly amend your ways and your doings; *if* ye throughly execute judgment between a man and his neighbour;

> *If* ye oppress not the stranger, the fatherless, and the widow, and shed not innocent blood in this place, neither walk after other gods to your hurt:

> *Then* will I cause you to dwell in this place, in the land that I gave to your fathers, for ever and ever.[231]

225 *The Church News*, "The words of Christ are the best 'why' missionaries need, Elder Holland says." Posted June 26, 2021, by Sidney Walker.
226 D&C 123:17.

227 "We Can Do Better and Be Better," *Ensign*, May 2019, 67.
228 D&C 19:4, 16–17.
229 See Jeremiah 6:13, 17, 28.
230 Jeremiah 7:2–3.
231 Jeremiah 7:5–7; emphasis added.

When it comes to repentance, one of my favorite quotes is from President Lorenzo Snow. He taught, "Do not expect to become perfect at once. If you do, you will be disappointed. Be better today than you were yesterday, and be better tomorrow than you are today. The temptations that perhaps partially overcome us today, let them not overcome us so far tomorrow. Thus continue to be a little better day by day; and do not let your life wear away without accomplishing good to others as well as to ourselves."[232]

As you go throughout your week, I invite you to be . . .

B etter

T oday

T han

Y esterday

---

232 *Teachings of Presidents of the Church: Lorenzo Snow* (2012), 103.

OCTOBER 17–23
"I WILL TURN THEIR MOURNING INTO JOY"
JEREMIAH 30–33; 36; LAMENTATIONS 1; 3

God's Message to Me from This Section

JEREMIAH 31:31–34—CHARACTER, COVENANTS, CHRIST (10 MINUTES)

Begin your study this week by watching "Like Him," performed by Aaliyah Rose.

(or google "Like Him—Aaliyah Rose Youth Music Festival 2020")

I know that covenants are described as a two-way contract between us and God. Although this definition is instructive, it doesn't bring much spiritual power to me personally. Honestly, I don't want a contract with my Father in Heaven. I want a relationship. My favorite scripture about the relational power of covenants is in Jeremiah 31. After describing a new covenant with the house of Israel, the Lord explains, "This shall be the covenant that I will make with the house of Israel; After those days, saith the Lord, I will put my law in their inward parts, and write it in their hearts; and will be their God, and they shall be my people. And they shall teach no more every man his neighbour, and every man his

brother, saying, Know the Lord: for they shall all know me, from the least of them unto the greatest of them, saith the Lord: for I will forgive their iniquity, and I will remember their sin no more."[233]

There is no talk of contracts in these verses. The covenant relationship is explained using relationship language, such as "inward parts," "hearts," "I will be their God, and they shall be my people," "they shall all know me from the least . . . unto the greatest," "for I will forgive them."

A covenant relationship with Christ allows us to know Him, learn from Him, and be like Him. President Ezra Taft Benson understood this relationship when he taught: "Men and women who turn their lives over to God will discover that He can make a lot more out of their lives than they can. He will deepen their joys, expand their vision, quicken their minds, strengthen their muscles, lift their spirits, multiply their blessings, increase their opportunities, comfort their souls, raise up friends, and pour out peace."[234]

I love the verbs *deepen, expand, quicken, strengthen, lift, multiply, increase, comfort, raise up,* and *pour.* Reread the

---

233 Jeremiah 31:33–34.
234 "Jesus Christ—Gifts and Expectations," *Ensign,* December 1988, 4.

quote, and underline the blessings you have experienced. When you are done, circle one of the prophetic promises you need the most right now. During your prayers, I would invite you to express gratitude for these specific blessings and beg for the blessing you need.

To summarize, finish this sentence in as many ways as you can: Having a covenant relationship with Jesus Christ means . . .

LAMENTATIONS 1; 3—SPLAGCHNIZOMAI (15 MINUTES)

If you could pick only one, which attribute of Jesus Christ is most important to you and why?

Attribute of Jesus	Why?

Now add the following:

Example of this attribute from scripture	Example of this attribute from my life

Here is how I would fill out these boxes:

Attribute of Jesus	Why?
compassion	In the New Testament, Christ's compassion is almost always expressed as the Greek verb *splagchnizomai*, which is translated, "moved with compassion." It is important for me to have a testimony that Christ's compassion is what motivated Him to action. Compassion is active, not passive. Compassion is dynamic, not static.

Example of this attribute from scripture	Example of this attribute from my life
At the beginning of Matthew 14, Jesus just learned that His cousin and lifelong friend, John the Baptist, had been unjustly beheaded by Herod. Jesus responded by going "into a desert place apart." It would seem He wanted some alone time to grieve. In His grief, "Jesus went forth, and saw a great multitude, and was *moved with compassion toward them, and he healed their sick.*"[235] What's even more shocking is that the next thing Jesus did was miraculously feed all of them, a count of "five thousand men, beside women and children."[236] Even while personally grieving, Jesus still helped where He could.	There are so many people going through so many heartbreaking experiences. I imagine Jesus grieving a lot for them. Even while He is grieving because of the painful suffering of so many others in the world, I still feel His compassion for me. One of the compassionate gifts He gives me is hope. Often when I pray or read my scriptures, I am filled with other-worldly hope. This is important to me because anxiety and depression make it more natural for me to feel hopeless. Even as I'm writing this section right now, I can feel the compassion of Christ through His motivating hope.

Jeremiah also wrote the book of Lamentations. The word *Lamentation* signifies deep sorrow and grief. Like someone in therapy because of trauma, Jeremiah journals about the grief he felt because of the destruction and scattering of his people. Because they would not hearken, Jesus could not protect them from the overwhelming power of the Babylonians. Even though the Israelites were suffering tremendous trauma, Lamentations balances the grief with a Savior who is *splagchnizomai*, or moved with compassion.

---

235 Matthew 14:14–15; emphasis added.
236 Matthew 14:21.

Mark the words and phrases that are evidence of trauma, loss, and grief because of generations of wickedness.

- Lamentations 1:1–3

- Lamentations 3:46–54

Mark the words and phrases that are evidence of Christ's compassionate character because of His eternal love.

- Lamentations 3:19–26

- Lamentations 3:55–64

Here is a simple summary of doctrines and principles from Lamentations:

- Because the Lord is compassionate, we can find hope in knowing He will help us if we seek Him.

- Jesus Christ feels both grief and compassion for us. In fact, His grief and compassion work together, motivating Him to never give up on us.

- The additional afflictions we experience because of sin and rebellion can help motivate us to turn again to the Lord if we let them.

- As we try to live a covenant relationship with Christ, our lives will be much more fulfilling than they would be if we chose to rebel against Him.

OCTOBER 24–30
"A NEW SPIRIT WILL I PUT WITHIN YOU"
EZEKIEL 1–3; 33–34; 36–37; 47

God's Message to Me from This Section

MY PERSONAL PLEA (1 MINUTE)

If I were to pick only one section for you to read from this entire book, it would be this one! I've taken more time and energy here than any other section in this book because many of the doctrines taught in Ezekiel are most relevant in our day. The purposes of these doctrines are meant to find us when we are lost, seal us to Christ in personal and transcendent ways, provide stability in a world marked by instability, and provide heavenly hope in our complex family relationships. The name *Ezekiel* means "God will strengthen." The book of Ezekiel is evidence that Jesus Christ is working many of His greatest miracles through The Church of Jesus Christ of Latter-day Saints. I plead with you to take the time necessary to work through this section.

EZEKIEL AND LEHI (5 MINUTES)

"Ezekiel was a priest who was among the Jewish captives carried away to Babylon by King Nebuchadnezzar in approximately 597 B.C. (see Ezekiel 1:3). According to the account in 2 Kings 24:14–16, the Babylonians took captive mostly the chief men of the land at that time. Therefore, it is possible that Ezekiel came from a prominent and influential family (see Bible Dictionary, "Ezekiel"). Ezekiel prophesied and delivered the Lord's words to the Jewish exiles in Babylon at about the same time that Jeremiah was prophesying in Judah and Daniel was prophesying in the Babylonian court."[237]

There are some striking similarities between Ezekiel and Lehi:

The first experience documented in scripture for both was a vision of God sitting upon his throne.	Ezekiel 1:26–28 1 Nephi 1:8
Both were given a book in a heavenly vision that talked about the devastations in Jerusalem and specifics about their personal ministries.	Ezekiel 2:9–10; 3:1–7 1 Nephi 1:11–13
Ezekiel prophesied of the stick of Joseph, Lehi and his descendants fulfill this prophecy by the coming forth of the Book of Mormon in the last days.	Ezekiel. 37:15–17 2 Nephi 29:6–9

---

237 *Old Testament Seminary Teacher Manual*, "Introduction to the Book of Ezekiel" (Church Educational System manual), 2015.

EZEKIEL'S OBJECT LESSONS ARE AWESOME! (15 MINUTES)

Do you have a favorite teacher? Who was it? What did they do to have such a positive influence in your life? What did they do in class to create a culture of learning?

In my opinion, Ezekiel would be the most engaging seminary teacher of all the Old Testament prophets. I can't wait to take a class from him during the Millennium. He is a powerful testifier, is courageous, and has a deep relationship with Jesus Christ. Oh, and his object lessons are epic! Here are some examples:[238]

Scripture	Ezekiel's Action	Possible Meaning
2:9–3:3	Ezekiel eats a roll of a book	Ezekiel internalizes the message
4:1–8	Ezekiel lays siege to a "tile" of Jerusalem	The Babylonians will besiege Jerusalem
4:9–13	Ezekiel eats defiled food	The Jews will have to eat nonkosher food as they are forced to live among the gentiles
5:1–4	Ezekiel cuts his hair and beard and splits the hair into three parts. One part he will burn with fire, a second part he will smite with a knife, the remaining he will scatter in the wind.	Israel will be burned, killed by the sword, and scattered abroad
12:1–16	Ezekiel packs his bags for a journey in sight of everyone	The Jews in Jerusalem will be forced to leave their homes
12:17–20	Ezekiel trembles and quakes as he eats in sight of everyone	The destruction coming to Jerusalem will cause a shortage of food
21:6–7	Ezekiel sighs, groans, and beats his breast	The news of what will happen to the Jews will make everyone mourn
21:8–17	Ezekiel slashes around with a sword	Jerusalem will fall by the sword

Your turn! See if you can find objects around your home that could teach someone the following:

- An object representing the spiritual culture where you live
- An object representing the scattering and gathering of Israel
- An object representing when we turn away from Christ
- An object representing when we turn back to Christ

EZEKIEL 37—THE BIG DIPPER AND LATTER-DAY SCRIPTURE (20 MINUTES)

Did you know that at least four temples have representations of the Big Dipper, or Ursa Major? (Because I grew up in the United States, I'm going to call it the Big Dipper.) The Salt Lake Temple is probably the most well-known, but it is also represented on the temples in Washington, D.C., Winter Quarters Nebraska, and Anchorage Alaska.

238 Adapted from Kerry Muhlestein, *The Essential Old Testament Companion*, 452.

If you can, take a few minutes at night to go outside to identify where the Big Dipper is located. For those of you who can identify other constellations, you could enjoy some additional time searching for and identifying those.

Understanding the importance of the Big Dipper in history will help you draw relevance and meaning from this object lesson. If you have children or teens, they will enjoy drawing the Big Dipper as you talk about the following:

• The entire constellation is made up of seven stars.

• If you draw a straight line through the two stars at the end of the cup the line will point you to the North Star (also referred to as the Polar Star, or Polaris). Using the North Star as a consistent bearing to travel at night has been essential for thousands of years.

• Stars in the night sky revolve around the steady, bright North Star. Although the Big Dipper rotates through the sky as well, it always points to the North Star!

Are you beginning to see the gospel parallels to these constellations? It seems that Alma the Younger understood the spiritual teachings of God's creations. During Alma's ministry, an anti-Christ named Korihor wearied him to show a sign of the existence of God. Alma testified, "Thou hast had signs enough; will ye tempt your God? Will ye say, Show unto me a sign, when ye have the testimony of all these thy brethren, and also all the holy prophets? The scriptures are laid before thee, yea, and all things denote there is a God; yea, even the earth, and all things that are

upon the face of it, yea, and its motion, yea, and also all the planets which move in their regular form do witness that there is a Supreme Creator" (Alma 30:44).

Donald W. Perry, professor of the Hebrew Bible at Brigham Young University, described three possible meanings of the Big Dipper on temples:

1. **Jesus Christ is the Creator**—Inasmuch as God is the Creator of all stars and constellations, it is appropriate that this prominent star cluster exists on several of His temples.

2. **Jesus Christ promises to find all who are lost and guide them home**—Just as the Big Dipper has guided navigators and travelers for millennia, the temple serves as a divine guide for us with regard to both temporal and spiritual matters. Through the temple, we can find our spiritual bearings as we navigate through mortality. Truman O. Angell, the chief architect of the Salt Lake Temple, explained that the Big Dipper's pointers always point to the North Star, and from this, we can create a gospel parallel that "the lost may find their way by the aid of the Priesthood."

3. **Jesus Christ is the way, the truth, and the life**—The Big Dipper points to the North Star, which is a symbolic representation of Jesus Christ.[239]

Hopefully, by now you are thinking, "This is great and all, but what does the Big Dipper have to do with latter-day scripture?" I'm glad you asked! Ezekiel prophesied in 37:15–20 that in the last days, there would be a stick (or book) of Judah and a stick (or book) of Joseph that "shall become one in thine hand." Most members of the Church know this prophecy is fulfilled by the Bible, the book of the Jews, and the Book of Mormon, the book of Joseph. Nephi saw the fulfillment of this prophecy in vision and taught the key purposes of the union of these books: to "witness unto you that I am God . . . that my people shall be gathered home . . . that I am God, and that I have covenanted with Abraham that I would remember his seed forever" (2 Nephi 29:8, 14; see also Ezekiel 37:21–28).

Notice how the Big Dipper is a cosmic testimony of this prophecy; in other words, the Bible and the Book of Mormon point us to Jesus Christ.

239 Adapted from, Donald W. Perry, *175 Temple Symbols and Their Meanings* (Deseret Book Company, 2020), 66–67.

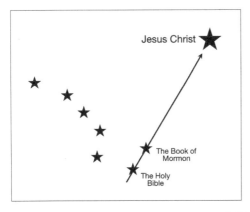

PROPHECY BEING FULFILLED ALL AROUND US (15 MINUTES)

Watch the following video describing Calyann's experience with the Book of Mormon. Just as Ezekiel prophesied over 2,600 years ago, modern scripture is pointing us to Jesus Christ.

(or google "Jesus Is Real: Calyann's Experience with the Book of Mormon")

Calyann's testimony of the Book of Mormon deeply resonates with me. Her faith in pressing forward anyway in the face of difficult questions is inspiring. Although we have different life experiences that have shaped who we are, the Book of Mormon has had essentially the same impact on us both. My assumption is that you had a similar experience watching her story.

The first book I wrote was a *Come, Follow Me* resource, like this one, except it was for the Book of Mormon. I concluded that book with my testimony of the Book of Mormon. I reaffirm that same testimony two years later.

> The Book of Mormon means everything to me. It is the most precious material possession I have. The Book of Mormon is like a doorway to another world. When I step into its pages, I find

God's love easier to feel and express. I find in it the answers to my life's questions, both past and present. I find a space filled with hope, love, light, truth, and excitement. But more than any of that, I have found my Savior, Jesus Christ, in the Book of Mormon. Maybe a better way to say that is, Jesus Christ has found me through the Book of Mormon. I know what it feels like to be found because of this book. Because of the Book of Mormon, I believe Jesus Christ loves to forgive me. I believe He can make me mighty. I believe Jesus knows what it feels like to experience life the way I do. I believe He loves to find God's lost children. Ultimately, I believe Jesus Christ is not only willing but is also perfectly capable of saving me and my family and anyone else who chooses Him. I believe Jesus Christ is worth worshipping in every way. I love Him with my whole heart, and I can't wait to see Him again so I can express all of these feelings to Him face-to-face as I am eternally wrapped "in the arms of His love" (2 Nephi 1:15).[240]

Please take a few minutes to have a short testimony meeting regarding the power of the Book of Mormon. It may also be edifying to write your testimony of this sacred book.

EZEKIEL 47:1–9—PROMISES THAT FLOW FROM THE TEMPLE (10 MINUTES)

Sometimes the scriptures make me laugh. One of the scriptures that always brings a smile to my face is Lehi's teachings of the divine purpose of the fall and the infinite blessings of the Atonement. I know it doesn't sound like a place in scripture where one would laugh, but it is! In speaking of the misery we experience because of the fall, Lehi taught, "And they would have had no children; wherefore they would have remained in a state of innocence, having no joy, for they knew no misery; doing no good, for they knew no sin" (2 Nephi 2:23). Notice the connection of having children and

---

240 *Come Follow Me through the Book of Mormon* (Covenant Communications, 2020), 144–145.

families to *misery*! Maybe it's funny because it's true. Maybe it's funny because it's sad. It's probably funny for both reasons.

Lehi knew, and it is no secret to most of us, that some of our greatest joy and misery is experienced within family relationships. Ezekiel had a vision of a temple. This vision has become the core of what I hold on to. In the following video, Elder Renlund and his family discuss the prophet Ezekiel's vision of the waters flowing from the house of the Lord. The river of water represents blessings that flow from the temples to heal families and give them life. It is very important to note that a modern seer is explaining and expanding on the vision of an ancient seer. The fact that there are multiple prophetic witnesses of the life-giving power of the temple cannot be overstated.

(or google "Elder Renlund and the River Will Grow")

To reiterate Elder Renlund's apostolic promise at the end, please read it and underline the aspects you need to hear most today.

> Brothers and sisters, I promise protection for you and your family as you take this challenge to find as many names to take to the temple as ordinances you perform in the temple and to teach others to do the same.
>
> If you accept this challenge, blessings will begin to flow to you and your family like the power of the river spoken of by Ezekiel. And the river will grow as you continue to perform this work and teach others to do the same. You will find not only protection from the temptation and ills of the world, but you will also find personal power— power to change, power to repent, power to learn, power to be sanctified,

and power to turn the hearts of your family members to each other and heal that which needs healing.[241]

Please read through Ezekiel 47:1–9 and mark every word that represents hope and life offered because of temple promises. Because temples are dedicated houses of the Lord that use His priesthood power, their purpose is His purpose: to bring life, hope, and healing to all the children of our Parents in Heaven.

Let me add a third prophetic witness to Ezekiel's and Elder Renlund's. John the Revelator wrote about his vision of life during the Millennium when mortal things have passed away, and we have "a new heaven and a new earth." Think of Ezekiel's vision of the temple as you read this verse: "And God shall wipe away all tears from their eyes; and there shall be no more death, neither sorrow, nor crying, neither shall there be any more pain: for the former things are passed away."[242] I believe one reason the river flowing from the temple in Ezekiel's vision needed to be healed is because much of the water was probably produced by the tears of broken hearts and broken promises in families during mortality.

What are some things you learned from Ezekiel that you hope you never forget?

What are some things you learned from the Spirit this week that you hope you never forget?

241 Elder Dale G. Renlund, Ruth L. Renlund, and Ashley R. Renlund. From a presentation at the RootsTech 2016 Family History Conference in Salt Lake City, Utah, USA, on February 6, 2016. To watch a recording of the presentation, visit lds.org/go/217Renlund. For a full transcript, see, "Family History and Temple Blessings," *Ensign*, February 2017.
242 Revelation 21:1–3.

OCTOBER 31–NOVEMBER 6
"THERE IS NO OTHER GOD THAT CAN DELIVER"
DANIEL 1–6

God's Message to Me from This Section

LET'S KEEP IT SHORT (2 MINUTES)

Many Christians are familiar with Daniel the prophet. Because of this, and because I was long-winded last week, my purpose is to be brief with the book of Daniel. My hope is to give you some content to direct your experiences while limiting my commentary. As you begin reading, it is important to remember that Ezekiel, Jeremiah, Daniel, and Lehi's family were all at the center of the Babylonians' scattering of Israel from approximately 610 BC to 587 BC. All these prophets were wealthy, influential, and extremely educated. All these prophets represent the many different places to which the Lord's people were scattered.

DANIEL 3—"BUT IF NOT" AND "FAITH NOT TO BE HEALED" (20 MINUTES)

Although disciples of Jesus Christ can expect the Lord to bless them in important ways, what, how, and when those blessings show up is entirely up to the Godhead. As Elder Jeffrey R. Holland once famously testified:

> I testify that this is Their true Church and that They sustain us in our hour of need—and always will, even if we cannot recognize that intervention. Some blessings come soon, some come late, and some don't come until heaven; but for

those who embrace the gospel of Jesus Christ, *they come.* Of that I personally attest. I thank my Father in Heaven for His goodness past, present, and future, and I do so in the name of His Beloved Son and most generous high priest, even the Lord Jesus Christ, amen.[243]

Elder Holland's testimony is exactly what the book of Daniel is about. In Daniel 3, we read a similar testimony from three Hebrew exiles, Shadrach, Meshach, and Abednego. When the outcome of their faith tragically resulted in the death penalty, they testified, "If it be so, our God whom we serve is able to deliver us from the burning fiery furnace, and he will deliver us out of thine hand, O king. *But if not*, be it known unto thee, O king, that we will not serve thy gods, nor worship the golden image which thou hast set up."[244]

Elder Donald L. Hallstrom of the Seventy gave a conference talk titled "Has the Day of Miracles Ceased?" In only ten minutes, he described how we can develop faith like Elder Holland's, the three Hebrews', and Daniel's—faith that transcends mortal outcomes.

---

243 "'An High Priest of Good Things to Come,'" *Ensign*, November 1999, 38.
244 Daniel 3:16–17; emphasis added.

(or google "Elder Hallstrom Has the Day of Miracles Ceased?")

Finally, here are two other examples in scripture that exemplify "but if not" faith using slightly different words. Can you think of others?

- Esther 4:16—"And so will I go . . . and if I perish, I perish."

- Luke 22:42—"Father, if thou be willing, remove this cup from me: *nevertheless*, not my will, but thine, be done."[245]

DANIEL 6:3–23—DANIEL'S LIFE TESTIFIES OF JESUS CHRIST (10 MINUTES)

As mentioned in previous sections, many Old Testament people, stories, and objects are meant to point us to and testify of Jesus Christ. For example, while in the garden, Adam voluntarily chose to give up his life so that we might live (see Moses 4:18; 2 Nephi 2:23, 25). The brass serpent, the blood on the doorpost during Passover, even the entire law of Moses "was our schoolmaster to bring us unto Christ" (Galatians 3:24).

The prophet Daniel is similar. The story of Daniel and the lions' den presents unmistakable connections to Jesus Christ.

Daniel 6:3	Daniel was set over the "whole realm" because of the "excellent spirit that was in him."
Daniel 6:4–5	The other presidents and rulers of the day hated Daniel, were threatened by his authority, and "sought to find occasion against [him] but they could find none."
Daniel 6:10	As the wicked leaders conspired against Daniel, he retired to a place where he "was wont to go" and there he prayed.

Daniel 6:14	Upon learning of the conspiracy, the king "set his heart . . . to deliver [Daniel]."
Daniel 6:17	As Daniel was sent to certain death, "a stone was brought, and laid upon the mouth of the den."
Daniel 6:19	The king arose "very early in the morning, and went in haste unto the den."
Daniel 6:22	An angel was present to assist Daniel in the lion's den.
Daniel 6:23	Daniel was ultimately "taken up out of the den and no manner of hurt was found upon him."

---

245 Emphasis added.

NOVEMBER 7–13
"I WILL LOVE THEM FREELY"
HOSEA 1–6; 10–14; JOEL

God's Message to Me from This Section

APPROACHING DIFFICULT SYMBOLISM (15 MINUTES)

The book of Hosea can be difficult to read primarily because it centers on a marriage between a prophet named Hosea and a whore named Gomer. While reading this story 2,700 year later, we may misinterpret the Lord's intentions. Rather than a story of sexism meant to prove the subservience of women, maybe we can read it as a love story centered in a complicated relationship. My purpose is not to defend the problematic implications; rather, my hope is that a love story between Jesus and His people will emerge and take center stage.

To understand the culture of Hosea, we need to go back in time approximately 150 years from Jeremiah, Lehi, Ezekiel, and Daniel to around 750 BC. Hosea is unique in that he lived in the Northern Kingdom of Israel and prophesied just before Isaiah. Therefore, the cultural issues Isaiah wrote extensively about can reasonably be attributed to the culture during Hosea's ministry.

In Hosea 12:10, the Lord taught, "I have also spoken by the prophets, and I have multiplied visions, and used *similitudes*, by the ministry of the prophets."[246] Let me explain the underlying storyline while incorporating some basic *similitudes* in the book of Hosea:

Hosea, a prophet, was commanded to marry Gomer (Hosea 1:2–3)	Jesus Christ, the Savior, who submits to the will of the Father by lovingly and loyally reaching out to Heavenly Father's rebellious children. This relationship is to be made by covenant. These rebellious and betrayed relationships can be redeemed only through loving kindness and longsuffering (see 1 Nephi 19:9).
Gomer, a prostitute, struggles to be faithful to Hosea. (Hosea 2:5)	God's covenant people, who consistently choose to be disloyal in their covenant relationship with Him. They seek other "lovers" in the form of lesser gods (see Doctrine and Covenants 1:16). Jesus alluded to this when He exclaimed, "For what shall it profit a man, if he shall gain the whole world, and lose his own soul? Or what shall a man give in exchange for his soul?" (Mark 8:36–37).

---

246 Emphasis added.

Marriage	The deep commitment, loyalty, reliance, and fulfillment that comes from our most important relationship. Many scriptures refer to Christ as the bridegroom and His Church as the bride. This imagery is the foundation of the parable of the ten virgins. Christ's Church is composed of both wise and foolish virgins. He is the bridegroom that brings redemption (see Matthew 25:1–13).
Whoredoms	Our willingness to sell our divinity and eternal promises for temporary mortal counterfeits and vain imaginations. It is important to point out that in scripture, whoredoms refer to *any* serious rebellion toward God. Whoredoms, therefore, are about much more than sexual rebellion. In Lehi's vision of the tree of life, whoredoms are anything represented by the river of filthiness and the great and spacious building (see 1 Nephi 8:26–27; 12:17–19).

The marriage metaphor in this book is important because it highlights the significance of our personal relationship with Christ. It also highlights the very real sadness, loneliness, and consequences of being disloyal to the covenant. Finally, it is important to point out that we are not sure if Hosea's marriage to Gomer was literal or allegorical, but the details of the book lead us to believe that it was more likely a literal marriage.

Okay, so what can we learn from this? We must always keep in mind that Gomer represents all of us! Because of the fall, "all have sinned, and come short of the glory of God" (Romans 3:23). When we take this truth too far, however, we may think we have out-sinned the Atonement, meaning we are beyond saving. Elder Dieter F. Uchtdorf used the following airplane analogy to ensure we understand it is never too late to come back. There is no such thing as a "point of no return" in our relationship with Jesus Christ.

[Airplane] flights over huge oceans, crossing extensive deserts, and connecting continents need careful planning to ensure a safe arrival at the planned destination. Some of these nonstop flights can last up to 14 hours and cover almost 9,000 miles.

There is an important decision point during such long flights commonly known as the *point of safe return*. Up to this point the aircraft has enough fuel to turn around and return safely to the airport of departure. Having passed the point of safe return, the captain has lost this option and has to continue on. That is why this point is often referred to as the *point of no return*. . . .

Satan wants us to think that when we have sinned we have gone past a "point of no return"—that it is too late to change our course.[247]

Have you ever felt like you have passed the point of no return with Jesus Christ? Often, this lie can take root inside of us due to circumstances and experiences in life that have very little to do with our intention to rebel against God. Last week, we read about Daniel ending up in a den of lions. Daniel did not end up there because he rebelled against God. He ended up there because that circumstance happened to him. And because we have his experience, it has become incredibly symbolic for us. Being trapped in our lions' dens in our day can mean we feel fear, loneliness, estrangement, hopelessness, and inadequacy. Sometimes our lions' den experiences are due to our own rebellions, and sometimes they just happen to us. Either way, there are parallels from Daniel's story to us just as there are parallels from Gomer's story to us. Gomer represents the struggles of covenant Israel to remember their identity and purpose.

HOSEA 2–14—OUR PERSONAL LOVE STORY WITH JESUS (15 MINUTES)

Here are some famous quotes from popular movies that reflect love and friendship. Using the information below, match the movie quote with the correct movie.

QUOTES

A. "Love is putting someone else's needs before yours . . . Some people are worth melting for."

247 "Point of Safe Return," *Ensign*, May 2007, 99.

B. "Death cannot stop true love. All it can do is delay it for a while."

C. "I can't carry it for you, but I can carry you."

D. "You have bewitched me, body and soul, and I love . . . I love . . . I love you."

E. "Only a true friend would be that truly honest."

F. "I'm also just a girl, standing in front of a boy, asking him to love her."

G. "It would be a privilege to have my heart broken by you."

MOVIES

1. Mr. Darcy from *Pride and Prejudice* (2005) _____

2. Gus from *The Fault in Our Stars* (2014) _____

3. Westley from *The Princess Bride* (1987) _____

4. Anna Scott from *Notting Hill* (1999) _____

5. Olaf from *Frozen* (2013) _____

6. Sam from *The Lord of the Rings: The Return of the King* (2003) _____

7. Donkey from *Shrek* (2001) _____

(Answers: 1. D; 2. G; 3. B; 4. F; 5. A; 6. C; 7. E)

While studying the book of Hosea, an important theme emerges: Jesus is really awesome! The way He continually reaches out to us is evidence of His character. Just before He died, Lehi told his righteous son Jacob, "I know that thou art redeemed." Well, of course Jacob would be redeemed. He's such a great guy. He writes scripture, confronts an anti-Christ, and fights for the marginalized in his community. But the reason Lehi gives for Jacob's redemption has nothing to do with how awesome Jacob is. Paraphrasing only slightly, Lehi says, "I know that thou art redeemed, because of the *awesomeness* of thy Redeemer" (2 Nephi 2:3). Jacob's redemption had nothing to do with Jacob. Therefore, we can transfer this same reasoning to ourselves. Like Jacob, we are all redeemed because of the goodness of Christ.

Read the following verses about how Jesus responds to us even when we constantly turn away from Him. These are expressions of love to us from our Savior.

• Hosea 2:14—"I will invite her back."

• Hosea 2:19—"I will betroth thee unto me for ever; . . . in lovingkindness, and in mercies."

• Hosea 2:20—"I will even betroth thee unto me in faithfulness."

• Hosea 2:23—"I will have mercy upon her that had not obtained mercy."

• Hosea 11:4—"I drew them with cords of a man, with the bands of love."

• Hosea 13:9—"O Israel, thou hast destroyed thyself; but in me is thine help."[248]

• Hosea 14:4—"I will heal their backsliding, I will love them freely."

To conclude Hosea, here is a testimony from President Henry B. Eyring centered on the teaching of Hosea:

> I had a new feeling about what it means to make a covenant with the Lord. All my life I had heard explanations of covenants as being like a contract, an agreement where one person agrees to do something and the other agrees to do something else in return.
>
> For more reasons than I can explain, during those days teaching Hosea, I felt something new, something more powerful. This was not a story about a business deal between partners. . . . This was a love story. This was a story of a marriage covenant bound by love, by steadfast love. What I felt then, and it has increased over the years, was that the Lord, with whom I am blessed to have made covenants, loves me, and you . . . with a steadfastness about which I continually marvel and which I want with all my heart to emulate.[249]

What evidence have you noticed in your life, your community, or in the world this past year that has helped you see how much Jesus loves us?

---

248 The Hebrew word used here for "help" is *ezer*, which is the same Hebrew word Jehovah used to describe Eve in Genesis 2:18. For a greater understanding of the significance of this word, see the section in this book for January 3–9, which covers Genesis 1–2; Moses 2–3; and Abraham 4–5.

249 "Covenants and Sacrifice" (address given at the Church Educational System symposium on the Old Testament, Aug. 15, 1995), 2; si.lds.org.

NOVEMBER 14–20
"SEEK THE LORD, AND YE SHALL LIVE"
AMOS; OBADIAH

God's Message to Me from This Section

The name *Amos* means "bearer" or "burden," referring to the heavy and difficult mission call given to him by the Lord to course-correct the kingdom of Israel. Around the same time as Amos, the Lord called Hosea and Isaiah to help carry this heavy message.

AMOS 8:11–12—I'M SO HUNGRY (15 MINUTES)

Take a few minutes and describe a time when you were hungry—like, really, really hungry. In what ways did this hunger impact your behavior? What words would others use to describe you when you are hungry?

Now brainstorm other metaphorical ways we experience hunger that don't include food. (Your list could include loneliness, illness, separation, disappointment, failure, insecurities, etc.) How have these experiences with hunger impacted your behavior?

Read Amos 8:11–12 and look for the way Amos uses physical hunger to prophesy of spiritual hunger. One way to define the word *apostasy* is to describe it as "a continual rejection of God's nourishment." Sometimes, we have the mistaken idea that there was only one apostasy and restoration that happened between the death of Jesus's Apostles and Joseph Smith. True, this apostasy was more global and far-reaching than others,

but the pattern of apostasy and restoration has happened repeatedly. Watch the following video to gain a better understanding of hunger and nourishment, or apostasy and restoration.

(or google "Dispensations: The Pattern of Apostasy and Restoration")

Here is a timeline of dispensations and historical apostasy that I have found very useful.

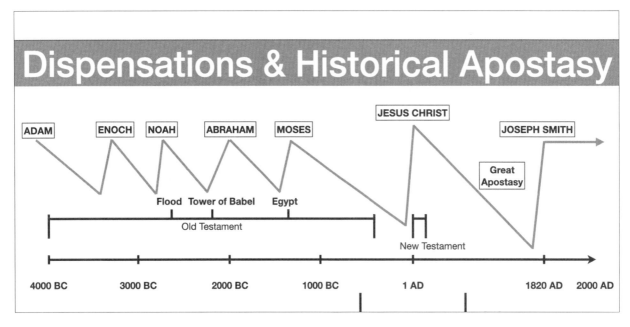

Dispensations & Historical Apostasy

As we focus in on the present dispensation, President Spencer W. Kimball declared: "After centuries of spiritual darkness, . . . we solemnly announce to all the world that the spiritual famine is ended, the spiritual drought is spent, the word of the Lord in its purity and totalness is available to all men. One needs not wander from sea to sea nor from the north to the east, seeking the true gospel as Amos predicted, for the everlasting truth is available."[250]

For most of us, experiencing hunger does not bring out the best version of ourselves. God obviously knows this, so He feeds us in a multitude of ways. Make a list of at least five methods God uses to feed you when you are hungry. In other words, how does God nourish and strengthen our bodies when we are hungry? (You're welcome for the Church culture humor.)

1. _____

2. _____

3. _____

4. _____

5. _____

AMOS 1–3—OBJECT LESSON! (20 MINUTES)

You will need three cups that are not clear. Gather enough small snacks for everybody, like Tootsie Rolls, Skittles, or Goldfish. Put all the snacks in one cup, but don't let anyone look inside. Let them know that they are going to vote for whichever one they think has the snacks inside. If they get it right, they get the snacks. If they get it wrong, they go hungry. Is everybody ready? Just before the vote, have one person come up and look inside the cups, but they can't say anything. They can only vote. Now have everyone vote for which cup they think has the treats.

- Did they get it right?

- What was the benefit of having someone who could see?

- What did it do for the confidence and hope of the group knowing someone could see?

- Did the group trust the one person who could see? Why or why not?

- How does this help you understand the role of having a seer on earth?

After an entire chapter prophesying of the destruction of major cities, including Judah and Israel, Amos testifies, "Surely the Lord God will do nothing, but he revealeth his secret unto his servants the prophets."[251] In the context of Amos's day, the secrets were centered around God's inability to protect people because they continually

---

250 Conference Report, April 1964, 93–94; see also *Old Testament Student Manual*, "1 Kings–Malachi," 3rd ed. (Church Educational System manual, 2003), 94.

251 Amos 3:7.

rejected His protection. But the secrets God revealed to prophets aren't always doom and gloom. For example, when we studied the Doctrine and Covenants and Church history last year, we were bombarded with God's latter-day secrets revealed through Joseph Smith, and they're awesome! Here are just a few:

- The true nature of the Godhead (see Doctrine and Covenants 76:22–24; 130:22; JS—H 1:17, 24–25)

- A global gathering of Israel (see Doctrine and Covenants 29:7–8; 110:11)

- Saving ordinances and priesthood keys (see Doctrine and Covenants 13:1; 84:19–20; 107:18–19)

- The plan of salvation, including the three degrees of glory (see Doctrine and Covenants 76)

- The restoration and role of the Church of Jesus Christ in the last days (see Doctrine and Covenants 20:17–37; 115:4–6)

Here is one secret President Russell M. Nelson revealed to help us manage our significant latter-day hungers:

(or google "President Russell M. Nelson on the Healing Power of Gratitude")

Through the rest of this year, I invite you to keep a gratitude journal. At the beginning of every section in this book, you have probably noticed a box titled "God's Message to Me from This Section." For the rest of this year, I encourage you to fill that box instead with gratitude. It could be people, things, experiences, God's hand in your life, etc. My hope is that you will fill your hearts with gratitude this holiday season.

NOVEMBER 21–27
"HE DELIGHTETH IN MERCY"
JONAH; MICAH

Experiencing the Healing Power of Gratitude

THE MULTIDIMENSIONAL STORY OF JONAH (10 MINUTES)

Jonah is one of the most fascinating characters in the Old Testament. You could make the strong argument, and many have, that Jonah represents the fear, prejudice, and pride we all face as mortals. You could also make a strong argument, and many have, that Jonah is a powerful representation of the mission of Jesus Christ. I am going to attempt to summarize Jonah in both ways. Wish me luck.

The story of Jonah began like many others in scripture—he was called by God to preach to a difficult audience. Like many others, Jonah was overwhelmed by his call. But unlike many others, he responded to the call by running away! "But Jonah rose up to flee unto Tarshish from the presence of the Lord, and went down to Joppa; and he found a ship going to Tarshish: so he paid the fare thereof, and went down into it, to go with them unto Tarshish from the presence of the Lord."[252] But the Lord saw something in Jonah and intervened. While Jonah slept, the Lord sent a terrifying tempest. Chaos ensued as the mariners prayed "every man unto his god"[253] for deliverance. No deliverance came. Then they cast lots to

see whose fault it was that God was so displeased with them. The lot fell on Jonah, and he confessed that he was running from the Lord. In his attempt to help these poor sailors, Jonah volunteered himself to be thrown overboard. So they did it! And it worked! "The sea ceased from her raging."[254] "Now the Lord had prepared a great fish to swallow up Jonah. And Jonah was in the belly of the fish three days and three nights."[255] All of this is in Jonah chapter one.

Chapter two tells the story of what Jonah learned in the belly of the whale, resulting in him returning to fulfill the Lord's calls to teach the people of Nineveh.

In chapters three and four, Jonah began to help the people repent, and the Lord poured His mercy upon these people. In a stunning scriptural turn, Jonah then complained to the Lord for His mercy upon a people who were known to be cruel. Jonah was so pained by the Lord's show of mercy to a people Jonah clearly didn't believe was worth saving that he declared, "Therefore now, O Lord, take, I beseech thee, my life from me; for it is better for me to die than to live."[256] The book ends with the Lord testifying to Jonah that all of God's children are worth saving!

---

252 Jonah 1:3.
253 Verse 5.

254 Verse 15.
255 Verse 17.
256 Jonah 4:3.

JONAH CAN REPRESENT DESTRUCTIVE PREJUDICE (15 MINUTES)

In the early years of his presidency of the Church, President Russell M. Nelson taught, "Today I call upon our members everywhere to lead out in abandoning attitudes and actions of prejudice. I plead with you to promote respect for all of God's children." In fact, it was in this very context that he pled,

> The question for each of us, regardless of race, is the same. Are *you* willing to let God prevail in your life? Are *you* willing to let God be the most important influence in your life? Will you allow His words, His commandments, and His covenants to influence what you do each day? Will you allow His voice to take priority over any other? Are you *willing* to let whatever He needs you to do take precedence over every other ambition? Are you *willing* to have your will swallowed up in His?[257]

Are covenant-keeping members of Christ's Church immune from the many forms of prejudice in the world? No! The scriptures teach that prejudice exists any time we view ourselves as better than others or any time we believe that another person or group is not worth saving. Here is a shocking but not surprising example from the Book of Mormon. After years of serving the Lamanites, Ammon called out the Nephites for their prejudices against the Lamanites.

> Now do ye remember, my brethren, that we said unto our brethren in the land of Zarahemla, we go up to the land of Nephi, to preach unto our brethren, the Lamanites, and *they laughed us to scorn*?
>
> For they said unto us: Do ye suppose that ye can bring the Lamanites to the knowledge of the truth? Do ye suppose that ye can convince the Lamanites of the incorrectness of the traditions of their fathers, as stiffnecked a people as they are; whose hearts delight in the shedding of blood; whose days have been spent in the grossest iniquity; whose ways have been the ways of a transgressor from the beginning? Now

my brethren, ye remember that *this was [the Nephites'] language*.[258]

Through discovery, service, and faith, Ammon and his brothers knew of the hurt and pain the Nephite prejudices caused the Lamanites. Of course, I'm not excusing the Lamanites fully here. My point is, just because the Nephites, or Church members, believed this about the Lamanites, *it did not make it true*! In fact, the Nephite prejudice was so bad that in the very next verse, Ammon told us the Nephites would rather kill the Lamanites than attempt to understand them. Ammon and his brothers, on the other hand, believed that all of God's children are worth saving. Ammon said, "We came into the wilderness not with the intent to destroy our brethren, but with the intent that perhaps we might save some few of their souls."[259]

Just like Jonah and the Nephites, if we carry around prejudices about people and groups where we would prefer to see them silenced, or worse, we are the ones in need of desperate repentance. It is also interesting to ponder that in spite of Jonah's prejudice toward these people, the Lord still used him to help others.

We can speculate about why Jonah felt a particular prejudice toward the people of Nineveh, but the real question for us is the same question the Apostles asked Jesus at the Last Supper when they were told, "One of you shall betray me." Their collective response was *not* to accuse the others in the room; rather, they responded, "Lord, is it I?"[260] In our day, it seems like President Nelson is saying, "Many of you are carrying around destructive prejudice." Instead of taking the easy way out by accusing others, prayerfully ask the question, "Lord, is it I?" In other words, "Am I willing to let God prevail over my prejudices of others?"

JONAH CAN ALSO REPRESENT JESUS CHRIST (20 MINUTES)

Like Jonah, none of us is 100 percent bad. Neither are we 100 percent good. We all travel throughout life somewhere in between. Like Jonah, some of who we are is not very useful and represents the difficulties and sins of mortality. Like Jonah, some of who we are is extremely useful and represents the healing and deliverance of Jesus Christ. Now let's analyze the aspects of Jonah that point us to Christ.

257 "Let God Prevail," *Ensign*, Nov. 2020, 94.
258 Alma 26:23–25; emphasis added.
259 Alma 26:26.
260 See Matthew 26:21–22.

First, Jonah is referred to as "Jonah, the son of Amittai."[261] *Jonah* means "dove," and *Amittai* means "truth." Therefore, "Jonah, the son of Amittai," means "the dove of truth." Much of the story of Jonah encompasses the three main images of a dove.

1. According to the law of Moses, doves were prominent in animal sacrifices. Jonah is offered as a sacrifice.

2. In the scriptures, doves are also considered heavenly messengers. Jonah is called as a messenger of God.

3. In the scriptures, doves are also considered a sign of heavenly peace. Jonah eventually serves as a messenger of peace and truth to the people of Nineveh.

Here is a table that shows how Jonah points us to Christ.[262]

Was a prophet from Galilee	Was a prophet from Galilee
Jonah was called to Nineveh, the capital city of Assyria. The Assyrians were known for their cruelty and overwhelming army. To go to Nineveh was to go to the most dangerous part of the world.	Jesus Christ was called to suffer at the hands of an incredibly cruel nation at an incredibly toxic time. Jerusalem at the time of Christ was considered the only "nation on earth that would crucify their God" (2 Nephi 10:3).
As Jonah attempted to flee the presence of God, he paid a fare to board a ship.	The Atonement of Jesus Christ required the complete withdrawal of God's presence for Christ to fully pay the fare for the sins of the world. This payment of debt from Jesus provided redemption from sin for us.
The violence of the storm and the cry of the mariners did not wake up Jonah from his sleep.	Jesus and His Apostles experienced something very similar during a violent storm.
They could not overcome the storm on their own, so Jonah willingly volunteered to sacrifice his life to save them and bring them peace.	We cannot overcome the Fall and the chaotic storms in our lives on our own, but through the voluntary sacrifice of Jesus Christ, we can find safety and peace.
God prepared a great fish beforehand to provide redemption for Jonah.	God prepared Jesus Christ beforehand to provide redemption for all mankind.
Jonah was swallowed up in the belly of the fish for three days and three nights. He would have been plunged deep in the depths of the dark sea.	Jesus Christ chose to have His will swallowed up in the will of the Father. In doing so, He was in the tomb for three days as He descended below all things on our behalf.
Jonah was reborn in the belly of the great fish.	Because of the sacrifice of Jesus Christ, we can all be reborn as new creatures in Christ.
After he was reborn, Jonah prophesied in Nineveh for forty days.	After Jesus Christ was resurrected, He prophesied in Israel for forty days.

Ultimately, Jonah is an unmistakable type for the voluntary death, burial, and Resurrection of Jesus Christ. Jesus Himself acknowledged this truth during His mortal ministry as a sign of His divinity to a wicked generation (see Matthew 12:38–41).

To conclude, read Jonah 2:1–10 and notice what Jonah learned about himself and the power of the Lord while in this tumultuous space.

---

261 2 Kings 14:25.
262 Adapted from Patrick D. Degn and Davis S. Christensen, *Types and Shadows of the Old Testament* (Deseret Book Company, 2018), 214–229.

NOVEMBER 28–DECEMBER 4
"HIS WAYS ARE EVERLASTING"
NAHUM; HABAKKUK; ZEPHANIAH

Experiencing the Healing Power of Gratitude

IS SUFFERING ALWAYS BAD? (15 MINUTES)

Nahum, Habakkuk, and Zephaniah all prophesied in Jerusalem around the same time as Jeremiah, Lehi, Joel, and Obadiah. Like their contemporaries, Nahum, Habakkuk, and Zephaniah urgently warned of the impending Babylonian takeover unless the people immediately chose to repent. The amount of powerful prophetic teaching at this same time is evidence of God's love for these people. However, as I read from Jeremiah through the end of the Old Testament, I often feel depressed. It's a lot of suffering, sadness, and desperation. From personal experience, I know that when these waves are continually crashing on the shores of my mind, it is easy to always feel overwhelmed. This is when reframing my perspective of suffering is important. Is suffering *always* bad? Watch the following video, and see if there's anything you learn from Lauren that can help you when suffering seems overwhelming.

(or google "Examining Questions with an Eternal Perspective")

Can you come up with three examples of when suffering has turned out to be an important part of your growth to become like God?

Example #1

Example #2

Example #3

MANAGING REBELLION (20 MINUTES)

Nahum's prophecies were mostly directed toward Nineveh. Before Jonah, Nineveh was not a reflection of goodness and compassion, but after Jonah's ministry to them, sometime between 790 and 749 BC, most of them changed for the better. When Nahum prophesied about 150 years later, it was clear that Nineveh, and the entirety of Assyria, had spiritually deteriorated to the point that the Lord could no longer protect them because they had rejected Him for so many generations. We know that Nineveh fell to the Babylonians in 612 BC. Immediately following this takeover, the Babylonians directed their full attention to conquering Israel, which they did over the next twenty-five years. This was primarily where the prophecies of Jeremiah fit into the narrative.

Is there a specific period of your life in which you were the most rebellious? In what ways did you rebel and why? Are you still in this period of your life? As you have moved through these rebellious experiences, what wisdom do you have now looking back?

Breaking the cycle of rebellion is one thing, but continually choosing to stay on the path is quite another. Nahum, Habakkuk, and Zephaniah can help us do both. I will approach these three books by answering two significant questions:

1. What do we do when we are stuck in our rebellion against God?

2. In what ways can the Holy Spirit bring "a mighty change in us, or in our hearts, that we have no more disposition to do evil, but to do good continually"?[263]

Three Principles That Answer Question #1

- Zephaniah 1:6–7—Even if I keep turning back to behaviors that aren't useful, the Lord will not give up on me.

- Zephaniah 1:12–14; Habakkuk 2:4—A life lived without Christ is far less fulfilling than a life lived with Him.

- Zephaniah 3:17–18—Even in my rebellion, Jesus Christ still views me as someone of value who is worth saving. He is still with me and has the power to save me. No matter how deep my rebellion is, He

is always there to remove my burdens, offer me joy, and bless me with rest in His love.

Three Principles That Answer Question #2

- Nahum 1:7—A personal relationship with Jesus Christ brings strength and trust.

- Habakkuk 3:10–11—In this chapter, Habakkuk used poetry to recount the Lord's past mercies given to those who trusted in Him. Verses 10–11 hearken back to the parting of the Red Sea and the miracle of the sun standing still at the conquest of Canaan. From this chapter, we learn the principle of sacrament, which is remembering that the Lord's influence in the past allows the Holy Spirit to give us strength and hope to overcome challenges in the present and future.

- Zephaniah 3:20—Jesus Christ not only has the power to deliver me from my burdens, but He can also help me stay out of captivity in the future. There is always hope.

As you watch the following video about Todd Sylvester, see how many of the principles above you can find.

(or google "The Hope of God's Light")

What is at least one principle you learned that could make a real difference in your life?

---

263 Mosiah 5:2.

DECEMBER 5–11
"HOLINESS UNTO THE LORD"
HAGGAI; ZECHARIAH 1–3; 7–14

Experiencing the Healing Power of Gratitude

HAGGAI—BACK TO WHERE WE STARTED (10 MINUTES)

If you refer all the way back to the section for January 10–16, I wrote the following regarding the importance of the question God asked Adam and Eve immediately following their transgression in the garden, "Where art thou?"

> In my opinion, this is one of the most useful questions in all of scripture. We too often ask ourselves where we want to go without first seeking to understand where we are! Even Google Maps teaches us this principle! If you type in a destination, you will never get directions unless you also enter a starting point. Usually, we use our "current location."
>
> When Adam and Eve partook of the fruit, Satan told them to cover up and hide, and they did. A loving Father soon arrived and asked them, "Where art thou?"[264] As far as I know, God doesn't ask many questions He doesn't already know the answer to. This question was not for Him. God knew where they

> were. This question was for Adam and Eve to better understand their "current location." Sometimes I wonder how long it took Adam and Eve to come out from hiding.

My invitation for you is to better understand your current location. Where are you regarding your relationship with our Heavenly Parents and Jesus Christ? Where are you in other important aspects of your life? In other words, speak your truth just as Adam and Eve spoke theirs so many years ago. Be real, be vulnerable, be willing to come out from hiding, and be honest.

_____

_____

_____

_____

_____

_____

_____

The very first words John the Beloved gave Jesus in His gospel was a question. When Peter and his brother

---

264 Genesis 3:9.

Andrew first begin to follow Jesus, the Savior asked, "What seek ye?" Considering what you wrote about your "current location," take a few minutes to write about what you seek or what you want this year as you study the Old Testament.

_____
_____
_____
_____
_____
_____

Haggai wrote during the time of Ezra, when the Persians allowed the Jews to return to their land and rebuild their temple. However, they became more focused on rebuilding their homes than rebuilding the temple. Through Haggai, the Lord spoke directly to their distracted behavior and invited the people to "consider your ways."[265]

If you completed the exercise in January, take a few minutes to "consider your ways" in December. Did you find what you were looking for? Where are you now? What's different, and what's the same?

Speaking of distractions, Elder Richard G. Scott made the following observation:

> Are there so many fascinating, exciting things to do or so many challenges pressing down upon you that it is hard to keep focused on that which is essential? When things of the world crowd in, all too often the wrong things take highest priority. Then it is easy to forget the fundamental purpose of life. Satan has a powerful tool to use against good people. It is distraction. He would have good people fill life with "good things" so there is no room for the essential ones. Have you unconsciously been caught in that trap?[266]

I invite you to "consider your ways," hopefully without shame or judgment but with genuine curiosity, to see if there are some good things that have distracted you from the essentials. If you are like me, the holiday season is a time when I become especially distracted from what is essential, which makes this exercise crucial at this time of year.

Good things that have become distractions	Essential things to refocus on

Finally, in much of the rest of the book, Haggai taught the people why rebuilding the temple first was more important than rebuilding their homes. As you read Haggai 2:3–9, notice how much his teachings focus on the temple as a dedicated space to feel the presence of the Lord.

ZECHARIAH—"THE DAY OF THE LORD" (15 MINUTES)

Write down at least ten words that describe the feelings and emotions you have when you think about the Second Coming. When you are done, underline the words you used that reflect dread and circle the words that reflect hope.

My Second Coming feelings and emotions

The content in the first half of Zechariah is like that of Haggai—they are both trying to expand the vision of the Israelites to focus their attention primarily on the temple. Instead of repeating a similar message, I want to look at the second part of the book, which focuses on "the day of the Lord."[267]

265 Haggai 1:5.
266 "First Things First," *Ensign*, May 2001, 7.
267 Zechariah 14:1.

"The day of the Lord" refers to two different time periods. One day of the Lord refers to the first coming of Jesus Christ and is described primarily in Zechariah 9 and 11. The second day of the Lord refers to His Second Coming and the events leading up to it and is described in Zechariah 10, 12–14.

One of the most interesting prophecies Zechariah gave of the first coming of Christ is Zechariah 11:12. This prophecy specified that Jesus would be betrayed for thirty pieces of silver. We know this prophecy was fulfilled by the fallen apostle Judas Iscariot.[268] Sadly, thirty pieces of silver was the price of an adult slave in ancient Israel. Nephi could also see the Jewish leaders at the time of Jesus: "And the world, because of their iniquity, shall judge him to be a thing of naught; wherefore they scourge him, and he suffereth it; and they smite him, and he suffereth it. Yea, they spit upon him, and he suffereth it."[269] Isaiah also similarly prophesied, "For he shall grow up before him as a tender plant, and as a root out of a dry ground: he hath no form nor comeliness; and when we shall see him, there is no beauty that we should desire him."[270]

Here are some Second Coming prophecies from Zechariah. As you read them, underline the ones that bring you dread and circle the ones that bring you hope.

Zechariah 9:11—Prophecy of the redemption of the dead in the last days. Of this, Elder Bruce R. McConkie explained:

> "By the blood of thy covenant"—that is, because of the gospel covenant, which is efficacious because of the shedding of the blood of Christ—"I have sent forth thy prisoners out of the pit wherein is no water" (Zechariah 9:11–16). "Wherein is no water"—how aptly and succinctly this crystallizes the thought that the saving water, which is baptism, is an earthly ordinance and cannot be performed by spirit beings while they dwell in the spirit world.[271]

Zechariah 12—The battle of Armageddon preceding the Second Coming of Christ. The Church's Bible Dictionary describes Armageddon.

> A Greek transliteration from the Hebrew *Har Megiddon*, or "Mountain of Megiddo." The valley of Megiddo is in the western portion of the plain of Esdraelon about 75 miles north of Jerusalem. Several times the valley of Megiddo was the scene of violent and crucial battles during Old Testament times (Judg. 5:19; 2 Kgs. 9:27; 23:29). A great and final conflict taking place at the Second Coming of the Lord is called the battle of *Armageddon*. See Zechariah 11–14, especially 12:11; Revelation 16:14–21.

Zechariah 13—The Jews will finally gain full forgiveness from the Lord (see Zechariah 13:6; Doctrine and Covenants 45:51–52).

Zechariah 14:3–9—Jesus Christ will fight for those who have taken the Holy Spirit as their guide. The healing waters will freely flow from the temple to heal individuals and families, and the Lord shall be king over the whole earth.

Elder Neal A. Maxwell understood the fear of the last days, but he also had a testimony of hope.

> Yes, there will be wrenching polarization on this planet, but also the remarkable reunion with our colleagues in Christ from the City of Enoch. Yes, nation after nation will become a house divided, but more and more unifying Houses of the Lord will grace this planet. Yes, Armageddon lies ahead. But so does Adam-ondi-Ahman![272]

268 See Luke 22:5.
269 1 Nephi 19:9.
270 Isaiah 53:4.
271 *The Promised Messiah: The First Coming of Christ* (1978), 241.

272 "'O, Divine Redeemer,'" *Ensign*, November 1981.

DECEMBER 12–18
"I HAVE LOVED YOU, SAITH THE LORD"
MALACHI

Experiencing the Healing Power of Gratitude

TEMPLE TALK (15 MINUTES)

In your opinion, what book or movie has the very best ending? What is it about this ending that makes it your favorite?

Similarly, having the book of Malachi at the end of the Old Testament, to me, is the perfect way to conclude the Old Testament because it points to Christ and His willingness to save all individuals and families throughout history. The last two verses in Malachi teach: "Behold, I will send you Elijah the prophet before the coming of the great and dreadful day of the Lord: And he shall turn the heart of the fathers to the children, and the heart of the children to their fathers, lest I come and smite the earth with a curse."[273]

This is the only scripture I can find that is quoted in all four of the standard works![274] The hope of Israel and all of God's children throughout history centers on Jesus Christ and is manifest in latter-day and millennial temple work.

Because of temple doctrine, we conclude that the vast majority of our Heavenly Parents' children will choose

celestial glory! My purpose is to connect Malachi with the further light and knowledge we have through Joseph Smith and latter-day temples. This is also the time when I need to remind myself of restoration doctrine that brings eternal hope when mortality feels hopeless.

Because of the Restoration, we know for a fact that the Final Judgment is *not* immediately following mortal death. Final Judgement is *after* a spirit world experience and an entire Millennium. From Doctrine and Covenants 137 and 138, we learn that the vast majority of humanity will choose a celestial lifestyle throughout eternity. You read that correctly: after the Millennium, Final Judgment, and assignment to kingdoms, the celestial kingdom will have the most inhabitants! Let me explain.

About three months before the Kirtland Temple was dedicated, Joseph Smith had a vision of the future inhabitants of the celestial kingdom. His brother Alvin was there, which surprised Joseph because Alvin died unbaptized at the age of twenty-five. Joseph marveled! How could this be? The Lord answered his question and gave us three massive groups of people who will walk celestial streets for eternity:

1. "All *who have died* [past tense] without a knowledge of this gospel, who would have received it if

---

273 Malachi 4:5–6.
274 See also 3 Nephi 25:5–6; Doctrine and Covenants 2; JS—H 1:38–39.

they had been permitted to tarry, shall be heirs of the celestial kingdom of God."[275]

2. "Also *all that shall die* [future tense] henceforth without a knowledge of it, who would have received it with all their hearts, shall be heirs of that kingdom."[276]

3. "And I also beheld that *all children who die* before they arrive at the years of accountability are saved in the celestial kingdom of heaven."[277]

Doctrine and Covenants 138:32–35 includes some of the groups above and adds another group: "Those who [have] died in their sins" will have significant time and experiences to choose what eternal lifestyle they want.

If you want your mind to be expanded even further on this subject, take some time to do the following study, which includes how billions and billions more of God's children will be saved in the celestial kingdom.

• Doctrine and Covenants 45:58–59—Will children be born during the Millennium?

• Doctrine and Covenants 101:28–31—What is life like for children during the Millennium?

• Isaiah 65:20–25—What other details do you learn about the Millennium?

Elder Bruce R. McConkie taught:

> Billions of spirits will come to earth during the Millennium, when Satan is bound, when there is peace on earth, when there is no sorrow because there is no death, when they will not be confronted with the evil and carnality that face us. They will grow up without sin unto salvation. Thus saith the holy word.

> Knowing this, we are obliged to conclude that a millennial inheritance is the kind and type of mortal life that billions of spirits are entitled to receive. Whatever the Lord does is right whether we understand his purposes or not. Without question there are many valiant souls now living who are worthy to receive a millennial birth, but who were

sent to earth in this day of wickedness to be lights and guides to [others] and to lead many of our Father's children to eternal life. But nonetheless, there will be billions of millennial mortals who will never be tested, as fully as we are, and who will go on to eternal life, as do little children, because an Almighty God in his infinite wisdom arranges that kind of life for them. The Lord gives each of us what we need. And, we repeat, the whole millennial system has been ordained and established to save souls. There is no other reason for any of the Lord's dealings with his children. He wants them to gain salvation, and he does for them what he knows they need done, in each instance, to hasten them along the way to perfection. . . .

> Truly the millennial era is the age of salvation. It has been established by the Lord to save souls. Truly he shall send to earth during that blessed period those who earned the right, by faith and devotion in the premortal life, to receive their mortal probation in a day of peace and righteousness. It is not unreasonable to suppose that more people will live on earth during the millennial era than in all the six millenniums that preceded it combined. And all those who live on the new earth with its new heavens shall be saved. The Lord be praised for his goodness and grace.[278]

THE TEMPLE IS THE PORTAL THAT CONNECTS THREE REALMS (15 MINUTES)

When I was serving a mission, I was perplexed for months by a simple question: Before the death of Christ, were there any temple ordinances performed for the dead? Using my limited study skills, I tried to find evidence in the Old Testament, the Gospels, and the Book of Mormon to answer my question. I couldn't find anything, so eventually I stopped searching. Less than a week after I had given up, I was reading in the Bible Dictionary, looking for something totally different when

---

275 Doctrine and Covenants 137:7; emphasis added.
276 Doctrine and Covenants 137:8; emphasis added.
277 Doctrine and Covenants 137:10; emphasis added.

278 "The Millennial Messiah," 660–661, 671.

the page fell open to the entry for *Temple*. The third paragraph had my answer!

> From Adam to the time of Jesus, ordinances were performed in temples *for the living only*. After Jesus opened the way for the gospel to be preached in the world of spirits, ceremonial work for the dead, as well as for the living, has been done in temples on the earth by faithful members of the Church. Building and properly using a temple is one of the marks of the true Church in any dispensation, and is especially so in the present day.[279]

As I have considered the far-reaching implications of the temple since then, an image has emerged in my mind. The mountains, tabernacle, and temples of the Old Testament were places where individuals could see the face of God. It was a connecting point between heaven and earth. But after Jesus Christ's ministry to the dead, following His own death, a third realm became connected. Now the temple is a place where mortals, spirits, and celestial beings walk the same halls. As far as I know, this is the only place on earth where these three realms connect. And so, it was always meant to be, especially in the last days.

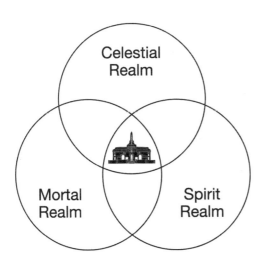

Significant evidence that President Russell M. Nelson is a true prophet of the last days is found all over in

his ministry, but maybe the most significant evidence is found in the following statement:

> My dear young brothers and sisters, these surely *are* the latter days, and the Lord is hastening His work to gather Israel. That gathering is the most important thing taking place on earth today. Nothing else compares in magnitude, nothing else compares in importance, nothing else compares in majesty. And if you choose to, if you want to, you can be a big part of it. You can be a big part of something big, something grand, something majestic!
>
> When we speak of the *gathering*, we are simply saying this fundamental truth: every one of our Heavenly Father's children, on both sides of the veil, deserves to hear the message of the restored gospel of Jesus Christ. They decide for themselves if they want to know more.[280]

It is my deep testimony that President Nelson has the vision of Malachi, Joseph Smith, and so many other prophets before him and is leading the charge to bring hope to Israel on both sides of the veil.

TEMPLE PROMISES IN THE LAST DAYS (10 MINUTES)

A good place to end our study of the Old Testament is with a brief analysis of the blessing that can flow into our lives *today* because temples dot the earth. As you read these promises, notice how many of them reflect our relationship with Christ and His desire to help us become like our Heavenly Parents.

Elder David A. Bednar promised:

> As you respond in faith to this invitation, your hearts shall turn to the fathers. The promises made to Abraham, Isaac, and Jacob will be implanted in your hearts. Your patriarchal blessing, with its declaration of lineage, will link you to these fathers and be more meaningful to you.

279 LDS Bible Dictionary, "Temple," 734–735; emphasis added.

280 "Hope of Israel," Worldwide Youth Devotional, June 3, 2018, Conference Center, Salt Lake City, Utah.

Your love and gratitude for your ancestors will increase. Your testimony of and conversion to the Savior will become deep and abiding. And I promise you will be protected against the intensifying influence of the adversary. As you participate in and love this holy work, you will be safeguarded in your youth and throughout your lives.[281]

Elder Richard G. Scott promised:

Do you young people want a sure way to eliminate the influence of the adversary in your life? Immerse yourself in searching for your ancestors, prepare their names for the sacred vicarious ordinances available in the temple, and then go to the temple to stand as proxy for them to receive the ordinances of baptism and the gift of the Holy Ghost. . . . I can think of no greater protection from the influence of the adversary in your life.[282]

Elder Dale G. Renlund gave us the "breathtakingly amazing" promises:

But as we participate in family history and temple work today, we also lay claim to "healing" blessings promised by prophets and apostles. These blessings are also breathtakingly amazing because of their scope, specificity, and consequence in mortality. This long list includes these blessings:

• Increased understanding of the Savior and His atoning sacrifice;

• Increased influence of the Holy Ghost to feel strength and direction for our own lives;

• Increased faith, so that conversion to the Savior becomes deep and abiding;

• Increased ability and motivation to learn and repent because of an understanding of who we are, where we come from, and a clearer vision of where we are going;

• Increased refining, sanctifying, and moderating influences in our hearts;

• Increased joy through an increased ability to feel the love of the Lord;

• Increased family blessings, no matter our current, past, or future family situation or how imperfect our family tree may be;

• Increased love and appreciation for ancestors and living relatives, so we no longer feel alone;

• Increased power to discern that which needs healing and thus, with the Lord's help, serve others;

• Increased protection from temptations and the intensifying influence of the adversary; and

• Increased assistance to mend troubled, broken, or anxious hearts and make the wounded whole.

If you have prayed for any of these blessings, participate in family history and temple work. As you do so, your prayers will be answered. When ordinances are performed on behalf of the deceased, God's children on earth are healed.[283]

My invitation for you is to follow the council of latter-day prophets, seers, and revelators to seek out your ancestors and then do what you can to have their temple ordinances completed. These blessings of *increase* are exactly what we will need to sustain us as the difficulties of the last days continue to *increase*.

---

281 "The Hearts of the Children Shall Turn," *Ensign*, Nov. 2011, 26–27.
282 "The Joy of Redeeming the Dead," *Ensign,* Nov. 2012, 94.

283 "Family History and Temple Work: Sealing and Healing," *Ensign*, May 2018, 47.

DECEMBER 19–25
"WE HAVE WAITED FOR HIM, AND HE WILL SAVE US"
CHRISTMAS

Experiencing the Healing Power of Gratitude

MICAH 5:2 AND MATTHEW 2:1–11—BABY JESUS (20 MINUTES)

Approximately 750 years before Jesus Christ was born, the prophet Micah gives a very specific and significant detail about Christ's birth. In fact, it is clear from Matthew 2:2–5 that the Wise Men who sought out the Christ child knew this prophesy: "But thou, Beth-lehem Ephratah, though thou be little among the thousands of Judah, yet out of thee shall he come forth unto me that is to be ruler in Israel; whose goings forth have been from of old, from everlasting."[284] Yes, this is a prophecy of the Christ child being born specifically in Bethlehem. But notice how Micah addresses the residents of Bethlehem, "Though thou be little among the thousands of Judah," signifying both the humble nature of our Heavenly King's birth and simultaneously testifying to the world that *no one is insignificant or forgotten to Christ.* Additionally, the word *beth* in Hebrew means "house of," and *lehem* means "bread." It is no coincidence that Jesus, the Bread of Life,[285] was born in Bethlehem, "the house of bread."

Please watch the following video about the birth and early life of Jesus Christ.

---

284 Micah 5:2
285 See John 6:48.

(or google "The Christ Child: A Nativity Story")

THE GOOD NEWS OF JESUS CHRIST RINGS THROUGH TIME AND ETERNITY (10 MINUTES)

Begin your study today with a powerful Christmas tribute to the King of Kings, Lord of Lords, and God of Gods (Revelation 19:16; Deuteronomy 10:17).

(or google "Chris Tomlin—Noel (Live) ft. Lauren Daigle")

This is a good time to review what you have learned about Jesus Christ, the God of the Old Testament. Read the following scriptures and mark every time you read something that testifies of the good news of Jesus Christ.

- Moses 7:53

- 1 Samuel 2:1–3

- Psalms 27:1, 4

- Psalms 35:9

- Isaiah 25:8–9

- Isaiah 51:11

- Isaiah 61:1–3

- Zephaniah 3:17

The Old Testament storyline really begins when Eve, full of divine wisdom, partook of the fruit of the tree of knowledge of good and evil. This year, we have studied many, many stories of how individuals, families, and societies have experienced the Fall and the Atonement of Jesus Christ. Therefore, it seems fitting to finish this book with Mother Eve's powerful witness of the good news of Jesus Christ: "And Eve . . . heard all these things and was glad, saying: Were it not for our transgression we never should have had seed, and never should have known good and evil, and the joy of our redemption, and the eternal life which God giveth unto all the obedient."[286]

---

286 Moses 5:11.

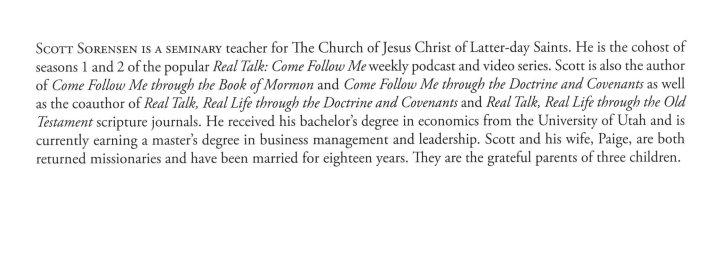

SCOTT SORENSEN IS A SEMINARY teacher for The Church of Jesus Christ of Latter-day Saints. He is the cohost of seasons 1 and 2 of the popular *Real Talk: Come Follow Me* weekly podcast and video series. Scott is also the author of *Come Follow Me through the Book of Mormon* and *Come Follow Me through the Doctrine and Covenants* as well as the coauthor of *Real Talk, Real Life through the Doctrine and Covenants* and *Real Talk, Real Life through the Old Testament* scripture journals. He received his bachelor's degree in economics from the University of Utah and is currently earning a master's degree in business management and leadership. Scott and his wife, Paige, are both returned missionaries and have been married for eighteen years. They are the grateful parents of three children.